D0989847

the american sportsman

Ridge Press & American Broadcasting Company Publication | New York | volume 3, number 3

Credits:
COVER: Photo by Arie deZanger. For details regarding historic lures and reels shown in picture, see "Afterthoughts" (p. 128).
Pages 28-29, 99: Collection of the Adirondack Museum, Blue Mountain Lake, N.Y. *Pages 31 (top), 105:* Remington Art Memorial Museum, Ogdensburg, N.Y. *Page 31 (bottom left):* "Alexander Mackenzie," from *The Frederic Remington Book*, by Harold McCracken; photo by Jack Richard. *Pages 52-59:* Photos of paintings for "Masterpieces of the Chase and the Catch" from Scala, New York and Florence. *Page 52:* Hunting Scene, by the Master of the Pollinger Panels; Alte Pinakothek, Munich. *Page 53:* Medallion of River Hunters, School of Giulio Romano; Palazzo del Te, Mantua. *Page 54 (left):* Self-Portrait in Hunting Costume, by Paolo Veronese; Villa Barbaro, Maser. *Page 54 (right):* Tapestry of Fishermen, by Francisco Goya; El Escorial. *Page 55:* Jolly Boat Towing Genoese Boat into a Bay, anonymous; Naval Museum, Pegli. *Pages 56-57:* "Hunt in Honor of Charles V," by Lucas Cranach; Prado, Madrid. *Page 58:* Deer Hunt, anonymous; Prado, Madrid. *Page 59 (top):* "Duck Hunt," by Pietro Longhi; Querini Stampalia, Venice. *Page 59 (bottom):* "Wild Duck Hanging in Two Views," by Jost Sustermans, Palazzo Davanzati, Florence. *Pages 67, 70:* Picture Collection, New York Public Library. *Page 76:* Antique reels from the collections of Virgil F. Pryor, H. C. Herndon, and Sam James. *Pages 102-103 (top), 102 (bottom left):* Collection of Maitland DeSormo, Saranac Lake, N.Y. *Page 102 (bottom right):* Collection of Atwood Manley, Canton, N.Y.

THE AMERICAN SPORTSMAN is published quarterly by The Ridge Press, Inc., 17 East 45th Street, New York, N.Y. 10017. Volume 3, Number 3, Summer, 1970.
EDITORIAL CORRESPONDENCE: All editorial correspondence should be mailed to 17 East 45th Street, New York, N.Y. 10017. THE AMERICAN SPORTSMAN will consider, but assumes no responsibility for, unsolicited material.
All submissions should be sent with return postage and self-addressed envelope.
SUBSCRIPTION CORRESPONDENCE: All correspondence concerning subscriptions, change of address, and undeliverable copies should be mailed to
THE AMERICAN SPORTSMAN, 2550 Huntington Avenue, Alexandria, Virginia 22303.
Single copies are $5.95; annual subscriptions are $20 in U.S. and Canada.
Second-class postage paid at New York, N.Y., and at additional mailing offices.
Printed in Italy by Mondadori, Verona.

STATEMENT OF OWNERSHIP, MANAGEMENT AND CIRCULATION OF THE AMERICAN SPORTSMAN (Act of October 23, 1962; Section 4369, Title 39, United States Code)

1. Date of filing: October 1, 1969.
2. Title of publication: ***THE AMERICAN SPORTSMAN.***
3. Frequency of issue: Quarterly.
4. Location of known office of publication: 239 Great Neck Road, Great Neck, N.Y. 11021.
5. Location of the headquarters or general business offices of the publishers: 17 East 45th Street, New York, N.Y. 10017.
6. Names and addresses of publisher, editor, and managing editor: Publishers, Jerry Mason and Fred Sammis, 17 East 45th Street, New York, N.Y. 10017; Editor Adolph Suehsdorf, 17 East 45th Street, New York, N.Y. 10017; Managing Editor, Robert Elman, 17 East 45th Street, New Y N.Y. 10017.
7. Owner (if owned by a corporation, its name and address must be stated and also immediately thereunder the names and addresses of stockholders owning or holding 1 percent or more of total amount of stock. If not owned by a corporation, the names and addresses of the individual owners must be given. If owned by a partnership or other unincorporated firm, its name and address as well as that of each individual, must be given.): The Ridge Press, 17 East 45th Street, New York, N.Y. 10017; The American Broadcasting Merchandising Company, 1330 Avenue of the Americas, New York, N.Y. 10019.
8. Known bondholders, mortgagees, and other security holders owning or holding 1 percent or more of total amount of bonds, mortgages, or other securities: Non
9. Paragraph for completion by nonprofit organizations; not applicable.
10. Extent and Nature of Circulation (A) Total number of copies printed (net press run): Average number of copies each issue during preceding 12 months, 50,000; single issue nearest to filing date, 50,000. (B-1) Paid circulation, sales through dealers and carriers, street vendors and counter sales: Average number of copies each issue during preceding 12 months, 3,000; single issue nearest to filing date, 3,000. (B-2) Mail subscriptions: Average number of copies each issue during preceding 12 months, 35,000; single issue nearest to filing date, 40,000. (C) Total paid circulation: Average number of copies each issue during preceding 12 months, 38,000; single issue nearest to filing date, 43,000.. (D) Free distribution (including samples) by mail, carrier, or by other means: Average number of copies each issue during preceding 12 months, 100; single issue nearest to filing date, 100. (E) Total distribution (sum of C and D): Average number of copies each issue during preceding 12 months, 38,100; single issue nearest to filing date, 43,100. (F) Office use, left-over, unaccounted, spoiled after printing: Average number of copies each issue during preceding 12 months, 11,900; single issue nearest to filing date, 6,900. (G) Total (sum of E and F—should equal net press run shown in A): Average number of copies each issue during preceding 12 months, 50,000; single issue nearest to filing date, 50,000.

I certify that the statements made by me above are correct and complete.
Jerry Mason, Publisher

contents

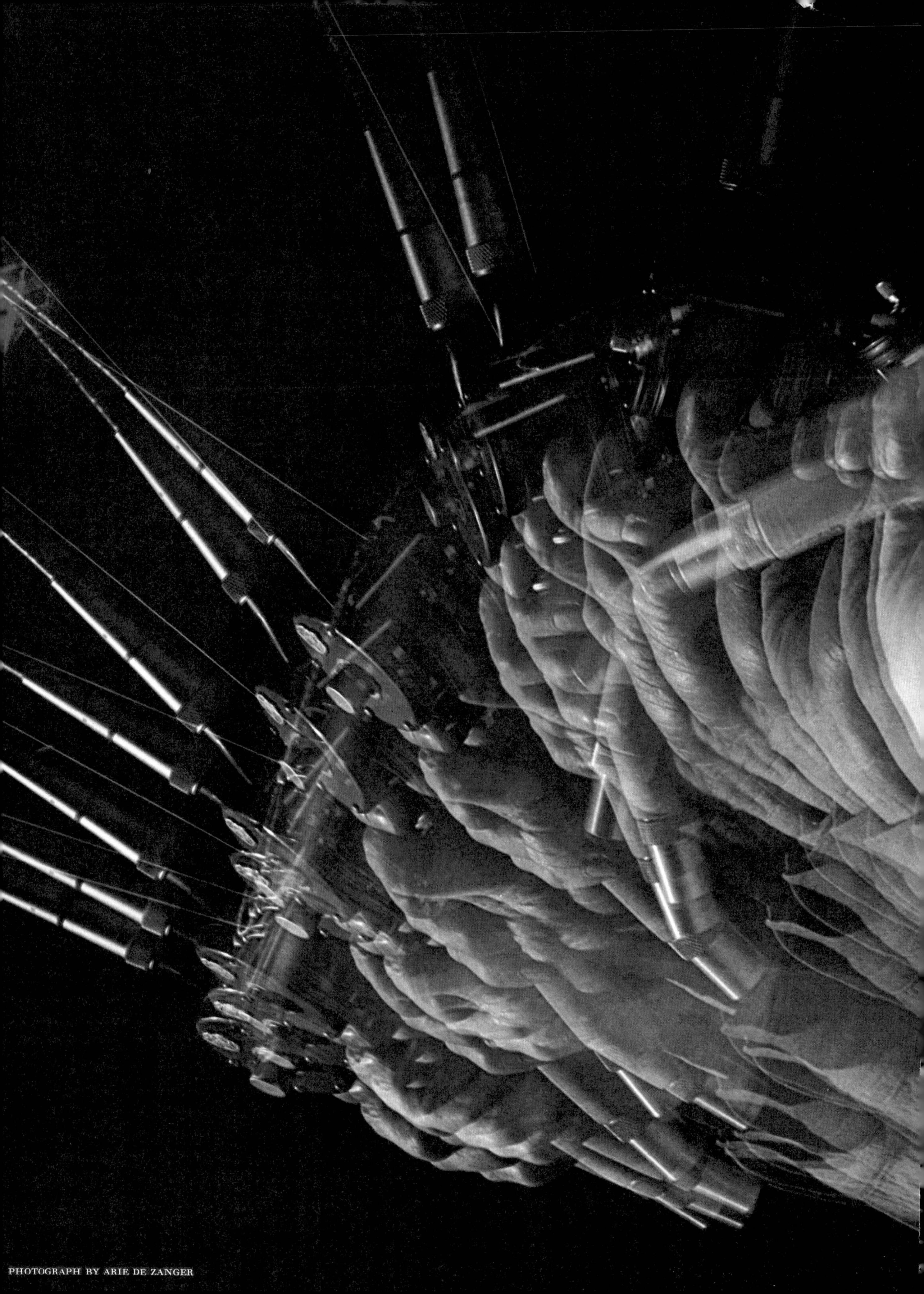

PHOTOGRAPH BY ARIE DE ZANGER

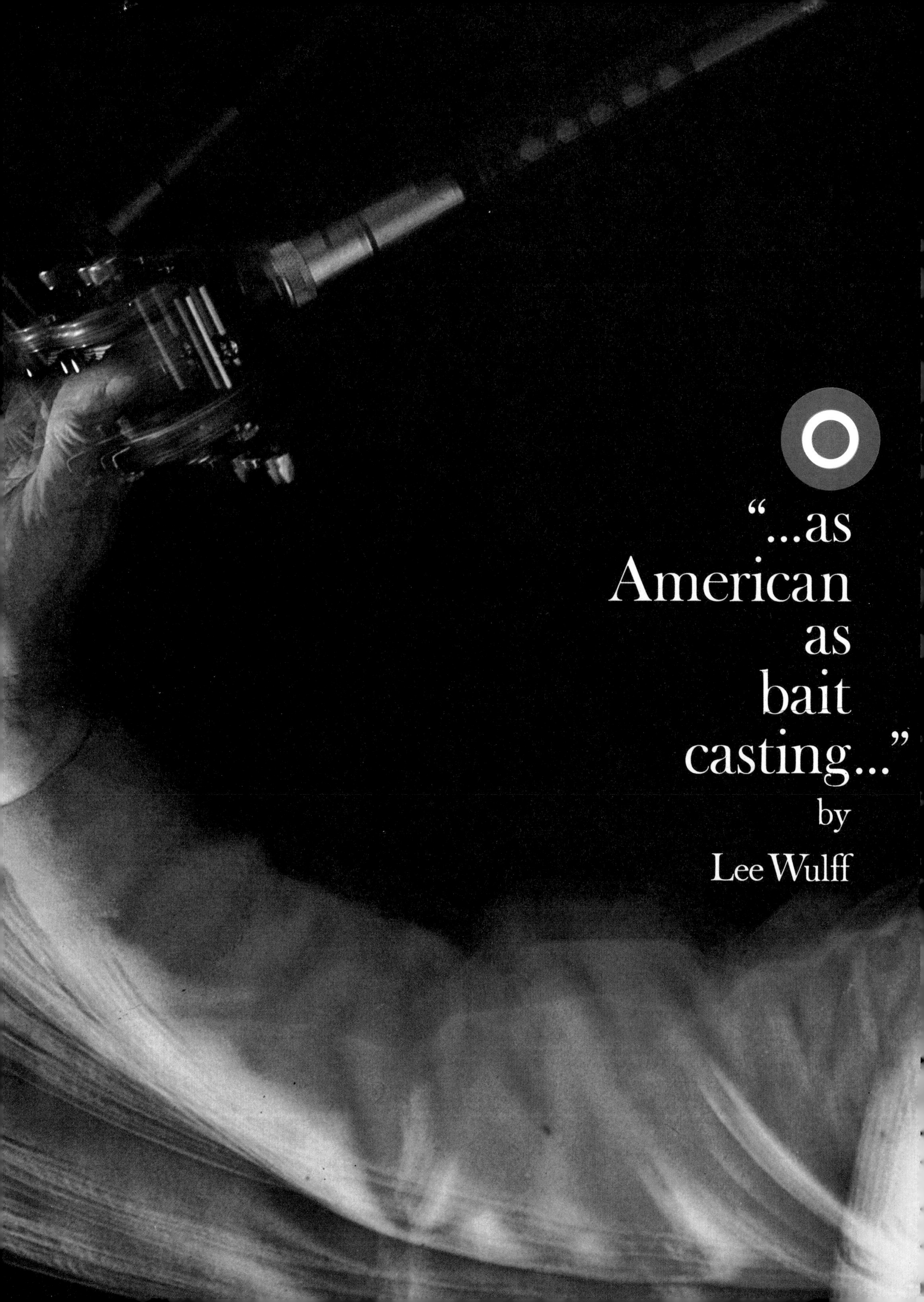

"...as American as bait casting..."

by Lee Wulff

Preceding pages: Author demonstrates smooth overhead cast, with reel turned sideways, wrist flexed, thumb over sp

Invented in Kentucky, where angling has always meant big bass, the multiplying reel led to better casting rods, irresistible new lures, and techniques that are still being expanded and refined today.

ERWIN A. BAUER

osite: Wading shallow Kentucky lake, angler battles acrobatic bass which struck plug during retrieve past weed bed.

As American as apple pie? One might just as well say as American as bait casting. Bait casting was born in Kentucky a hundred and sixty years ago and is truly American in concept and evolution. There were two major factors involved: the same ingenuity that made the Yankee Clippers the fastest ships on the oceans, and the pugnacity of the American black bass.

Until some Kentucky watchmakers started devising multiplying reels, bait casting as we know it could not exist. The invention of these light multiplying reels made it possible to cast a bait weighing from half an ounce upward directly from the revolving spool by having the weight of the lure pull the line off. Until then, casting of bait had been accomplished by manually taking the necessary line off the reel, coiling it carefully on the bottom of the boat, and making a sweeping cast that pulled the loose line out through the guides. The procedure was somewhat like fly casting. Under the best of conditions, sixty feet was a great cast.

For almost a hundred years after the first multiplying reels were made, this type of fishing continued to be done with live, or natural, bait and it is from this that the name "bait casting" was derived. The term is still commonly employed in connection with multiplying reels and the rods designed for such fishing, even when artificial lures are used. In these circumstances "plug casting" may be a more accurate designation, yet this synonym has never really replaced the original, richly traditional name for the sport. It was not until the early years of this century—when Jim Heddon put his Dowagiac plugs on the market—that bait casting made the final surge to its full dimension.

At the beginning of the nineteenth century, only two kinds of casting reels were available—the English single-action type which was generally made of brass, and the domestic wooden improvisation consisting of an old sewing spool mounted on a metal frame. Attached to a light, nine- or ten-foot wooden rod, either type of spool was no more than a convenient but awkwardly balanced holding spool for the raw-silk line to be manually unwound and coiled in the boat. It then took considerable skill to strip-cast a live minnow fifty or sixty feet. There was no other practical way to cast, since the inertia of the heavy brass or primitive wooden spool prevented line from being unreeled by the pull of a bait flicked through the air. And the reel was of little help in playing any fish that was hooked.

The development of the multiplying reel—utilizing a very easily turned spool that revolved several times for each turn of the crank handle—arose from a fortunate combination of circumstances. Its birth in Kentucky was as natural as the perfecting of fine hunting rifles had been in Pennsylvania. For one thing, big, belligerent black bass were so plentiful in Kentucky that it is little wonder Kentuckians were devoted anglers. For another, a number of fine watchmakers had settled in the area. The multiplying reel, both in concept and in construction, owed a great deal to the craft of building fine timepieces. For the spool to turn easily

on the cast, without manual stripping, gear wheels had to be ingeniously designed and shaped and cut with precision. Each part was painstakingly made by hand.

The construction of the first multiplying reel is credited to George Snyder. The year was 1810. In those early days all the reels had to be hand-made and carefully fitted. Parts, even screws, were not interchangeable. The Meek brothers, Jonathan and Benjamin, followed swiftly with reels featuring innovations of their own—a collar around the crankshaft, jeweled pivot bearings, a spiral gear, sliding buttons for the click and drag springs. Soon many Kentucky watchmakers began producing carefully designed, effective, and expensive multiplying reels. In 1840 a top-quality bait-casting reel might cost $75, as much as a fine fowling piece. Many of the early reels were so well-made that they lasted a lifetime and some are still around and in good casting shape today. Snyder built one for the Honorable Brutus Clay in 1821, and it was still being used seventy years later by Clay's son.

The first models were mounted on rods that were eight to ten feet long and weighed about seven ounces. Rods were made of greenheart, lancewood, bethabara, or one of many local woods that possessed the necessary combination of lightness and strength. The common baits were minnows, crawfish, frogs, and, of course, worms. The ease of casting by this method enabled an angler to make many more casts in a given fishing period. Casting became more productive not only by covering more water but because it permitted a fisherman to drop a bait more precisely on target—for example, into a pocket of open water in a bed of lily pads.

Although bait casting flourished, some of its devotees found cause for complaint. Many of them, fishing unsuccessfully with frogs or minnows, had been filled with concern and disgust when a big bass that had steadfastly refused their natural baits would strike viciously at a discarded cigar butt or an empty matchbox tossed carelessly into the water. This pugnacity of the bass, coupled with its voraciousness, made modern-day bait casting—plug casting—inevitable. History doesn't record the first angler

In film sequence from American Sportsman-ABC television show, Florida bass desperately tries to shake hook, first executing sharp turn and then surfacing in head-twisting leap. Action occurred close to boat, but fish had to be played for several minutes more before it was netted.

to catch a bass on a block of wood with a hook hanging from it, but around 1906 Jim Heddon of Dowagiac, Michigan, began making and selling artificial lures.

Just as artificial flies had proved to be a great boon to the trout anglers who had once carried live insects or worms in a bait box, so wooden plugs and metal lures opened up a better, brighter world for bass fishermen. Instead of finding it necessary to buy or catch an assortment of baits ranging from hellgramites to mice and then keep them alive and lively, it became possible simply to pick up a tackle box containing a few painted wooden plugs and go fishing. Until that time fly fishing had reigned supreme in the sportsman's esteem. It had elegance and delicacy which made it popular in the best circles, and the flies were *artificial*. Artificial lures moved bait casting up into the same general category.

At the same time, black-bass territory was expanding. Bait casting and bass were a matched pair; they prospered together. Largemouths, originally limited to the Midwest and the South, were becoming established throughout the nation. Smallmouths, limited in the beginning to the Lake Ontario and Ohio River drainages, were successfully transplanted to New England and the East

CONTINUED ON PAGE 73

HOTOGRAPHS BY ARIE DE ZANGER

Far left: Superb old lures in tackle box include 1915 Heddon Panatella (top row, fourth from left) and 1919 Schoonie's Scooter (red and white plug in lower square compartment), one of earliest surface-disturbers. Above: Shown with mahogany line drier and 1930 Creek Chub Jointed Minnow are Congress (left) and South Bend No. 300 reels made in Thirties. Left: Pictured with Utica reel of same vintage are very effective homemade Decker plug, c. 1920, and Pflueger Muskill feathered spoon, introduced in early Thirties.

Salmon and Caribou of the Ungava

by

Jerome B. Robinson

In Quebec's wild northland, where mornings are for trophy hunting, afternoons for trophy fishing, a man soon learns to expect the unexpected and to keep both rifle and rod always at hand.

photography by

Hanson Carroll

Soon after taking two fine salmon (below), author felled caribou near river's edge; he and guide brought trophy to camp in canoe (preceding pages). Photographer Hanson Carroll (right) caught several good fish in same large pool.

In the far northern reaches of Quebec, halfway between Hudson Bay and the southern tip of Greenland, is a sportsmen's mecca known as the Ungava region. Until a few years ago the vast area where pure rivers flow north to Ungava Bay was familiar mainly to nomadic Indian and Eskimo hunters and to geologists in the employ of mining companies. Today the name Ungava is murmured reverently by knowing outdoorsmen.

The mining companies opened up this subarctic region, and scheduled airlines now stop regularly at places previously seen by few white men. The airport at Schefferville on the Quebec-Labrador border has become a crossroads for caribou hunters and Atlantic salmon fishermen.

Failure to catch fish is unthinkable on Ungava salmon waters, such as the George, Whale, Koksoak, Leaf, and DePas rivers. Wealthy sportsmen who have sought the Atlantic salmon throughout its European and American range have reported that the angling in the Ungava region in July and again in September is the best they've ever experienced. In the seven years that the Ungava

Caribou are frequently seen swimming DePas River (left) during early morning and again in late afternoon. When prime bull pauses atop nearby ridge (below), clear silhouette offers hunter ideal shot.

has been open to hunters, ninety-four percent of those seeking caribou have come out with trophies.

The typical pattern in an Ungava sporting camp is to hunt caribou in the morning when frost whitens the tundra and fishing is prevented by icing of rod guides. By noon, when the weather warms, the caribou are bedded down in gullies of deep willow bush and spruce, and insects stir from the moss and lichens on the hillsides. You move down to the river and cast for salmon during the early afternoon hours. With the chill of dusk, the insect hordes are stilled and the caribou come down to the rivers to drink. It is time to hunt again. Conversely, salmon are notoriously late risers, usually ignoring flies before late morning. Since the fish are most active when the game is least active, caribou hunting and salmon fishing make an ideal combination.

The airport in Schefferville is strangely modern. The building is of metal and glass, and four-engined aircraft keep the muddy runway

CONTINUED ON PAGE 84

WILDLIFE OF EAST AFRICA

Armed only with a camera, a hunter-conservationist photographs dangerous game at close range.

Text and photography by Leonard Lee Rue III

The African sun was sickly yellow, its brilliance obscured in choking clouds of dust raised by thousands upon thousands of cloven hoofs. No rain had fallen in five-and-a-half weeks, and the vegetation on the plains of Serengeti lay brittle and dead. The high hills in the western part of the park act as a barrier, making the valley a funnel. Through this natural cleft the long strings of wildebeest issued and spread out like rivers of oil. As the wildebeest trekked, emitting a cacophony of short bleats and snorts, they paused now and then in a futile effort to find relief from the heat in the meager shade of the flat-topped acacia trees.

During the afternoon at least fifty thousand wildebeest passed by, plus countless zebras and a sprinkling of impala. It was a scene that I had traveled halfway around the world to see. Nowhere else can so many big-game animals, of so many varieties, be observed at one time as on the Serengeti Plains. The main wildebeest herd is estimated at some four hundred and

Title pages: Elephant herd shuffles by in trunk-to-tail formation. Above: Bull elephant leaves companions to rub against giant anthill. Top left: Cape buffalo luxuriates in deep wallow. Bottom left: Crocodile surfaces in Nile River.

Above left: Lappet-faced vultures settle near wildebeest killed by lions. Above right: Pied kingfisher hovers over water, seeking prey. Far right: Cape widgeon and greater flamingos rest and feed in shallows.

fifty thousand animals.

East Africa. I had been brought up on Frank Buck, read about the exploits of Martin and Osa Johnson, immersed myself in the works of Robert Ruark, Ernest Hemingway, and Bernhard Grzimek. I suppose most outdoorsmen of my generation have dreamed of seeing Africa. In the salad days of big-game hunting—the days of Theodore Roosevelt and Stewart Edward White—the wealthy and even the not so wealthy could manage an African trip if they really wanted to, and could arrange a leave of absence from their work. Then came a long, sad period during which the Dark Continent receded from the horizons of the traveling sportsman. Game populations had dwindled tragically as a result of uncontrolled hunting, natural disasters, and, in some areas, the spread of western-style civilization. Moreover, the pace of business and professional life had changed, and most men could no longer afford the time required by a long voyage and a safari. Finally, of course,

Far left: Rhino charges. Author took picture as guide put Land Rover into gear and began hasty retreat. Above: Lion reposes in tree at Lake Manyara. Left: Uganda kob bucks clash in battle over harem and territory.

wars and depressions put Africa still farther out of reach.

The face of Africa will never again be as it was, but much has changed for the better. Despite unrest among some of the emerging nations, a number of African governments have been able to inaugurate excellent game-control and conservation programs. In Kenya, Tanzania, and Uganda, some types of wildlife are again on the increase. And these countries have an economic interest in encouraging sportsmen to make safaris. Modern air travel and a proliferation of special tours have reduced both the time and the cost of African trips, and in this period of American affluence a great many sportsmen are once again able to turn their dreams into reality.

My own trip was somewhat unusual in that I planned to kill no game—none at all. Mine was to be a strictly photographic safari. Not that I don't hunt. I've taken my share of game in the United States, Canada, and Alaska, and I am chief gamekeeper for Coventry, a large

CONTINUED ON PAGE 93

Above: Scores of hippos cool themselves in muddy river, near banks where forage is abundant. Left: Hippo approaches shore. Animal's body is dark where it was submerged, lighter along sun-dried back.

A CRAFT FOR ALL WATERS

Since the days of birchbarks and dugouts, the swiftly gliding canoe has been ideal for navigating America's lakes and streams.

BY JOHN GARDNER

Preceding pages: In "An Anxious Moment," 1880 painting by A. F. Tait, hunters use birchbark canoe to stalk deer. Frederic Remington's "Howl of the Weather" (right) and "Alexander Mackenzie" (below) show birchbark and large dugout. Canoe in photo is Atwood Manley's "Vayu," famous old smoothskin-cedar type of craft produced by Rushton.

Once again the song of the voyageur is heard in the North. It is summer and the canoes are moving out, more this year than last, paddles flashing or dipping silently, trending into wilderness ways where the skies are bright, the waters clean, and the air tangy with balsam.

In selecting a canoe these days, one can investigate a variety of materials: aluminum, fiberglass, polypropylene, time-tested canvas, and a rubber-based plastic. But in essential shape all these modern canoes are closely alike, deriving from birchbark prototypes which have not substantially changed in design since the Old Stone Age.

Perhaps aluminum or some of the new plastic materials are tougher than bark, and will stand up to more abuse on flinty gravel or jagged boulders; yet each has its disadvantages. Aluminum is noisy, tends to hang up on rocks, and takes dents which refuse to pound out cleanly. Fiberglass is heavy. And so on. According to all accounts, the best of the old bark canoes would go just as far and just as fast as anything we have today, besides carrying just as big loads. The feats accomplished in birchbark canoes have been numerous and extraordinary.

Canoes are ancient in origin, worldwide in occurrence, and all but infinite in their variety. There are dugouts of every sort contrived from hollowed logs, a variety of frames covered with bark or hide, and still other species of canoe formed from bundles of buoyant reeds or rushes—papyrus on the upper Nile and balsa on Lake Titicaca in Bolivia and Peru. Size also varies greatly. The tiny cypress dugouts no more than eight feet long, twenty inches wide, and eight inches deep used by Creole frog hunters in Louisiana swamps, contrast with Haida war dugouts of cedar sixty-five feet long, with six to eight feet of beam, which once were not uncommon on our northwest coast. Even larger war canoes, worked out of gigantic logs of kauri pine with wash strakes added to increase the freeboard, were once used by the Maori warriors of New Zealand.

When white settlers first reached the eastern shores of North America, they found log

VICTOR SMITH

*eft: Time-tested wood and canvas
noe is poled over shallows of Allagash
ake in Maine. Below: Flyfisherman
sts from old birchbark. Bottom left:
berglass model competes in race.
ttom right: Latex canoe is maneuvered
er beaver dam obstructing river.*

ANSON CARROLL
ETER MILLER

LEONARD LEE RUE III

Aluminum canoe, pictured shooting rapids, is among more popular of modern types. Such canoes handle well, are stable, reasonably light, and very durable.

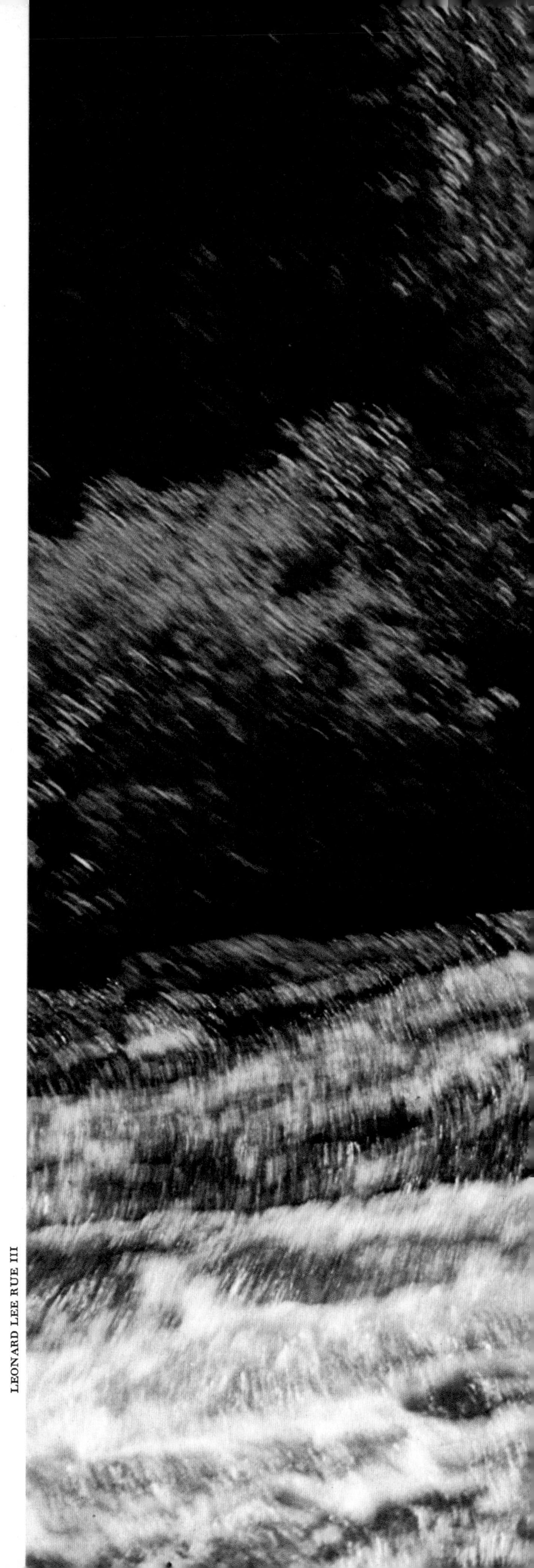
LEONARD LEE RUE III

dugouts, as well as bark canoes, with the former in common use along the entire Atlantic Coast. Such native craft were immediately adopted, though log canoes eventually were replaced by planked boats.

Robert B. Roosevelt in his book, *Some Game Fish of the North*, published in New York in 1862, mentions the white-pine dugouts of thirty feet favored by the salmon fishermen on the St. John River near Fredericton, New Brunswick. More than two hundred years earlier in Salem, Massachusetts, every household, according to Wood's *New England Prospect*, had one or more "small Cannowes, which were made of whole pine trees being about two foot & a half over, and 20 foote long." The villagers used these dugouts principally for going back and forth to their farms, but also "in these likewise they goe a-fowling, sometimes two leagues to sea," probably to hunt ducks among the outer islands of Marblehead Harbor, as their descendants still do.

About this same time, Roger Williams was becoming acquainted with the dugout canoes of the Indians near Narragansett Bay, which craft he accounted crank and treacherous, having nearly drowned on more than one occasion while using them. When the first English settlers arrived at Southhold and Southampton at the eastern end of Long Island in 1640, they found the local Indians carrying on a flourishing whale fishery in log canoes. Some of these were large. One dugout belonging to Chief Wyandanch

CONTINUED ON PAGE 98

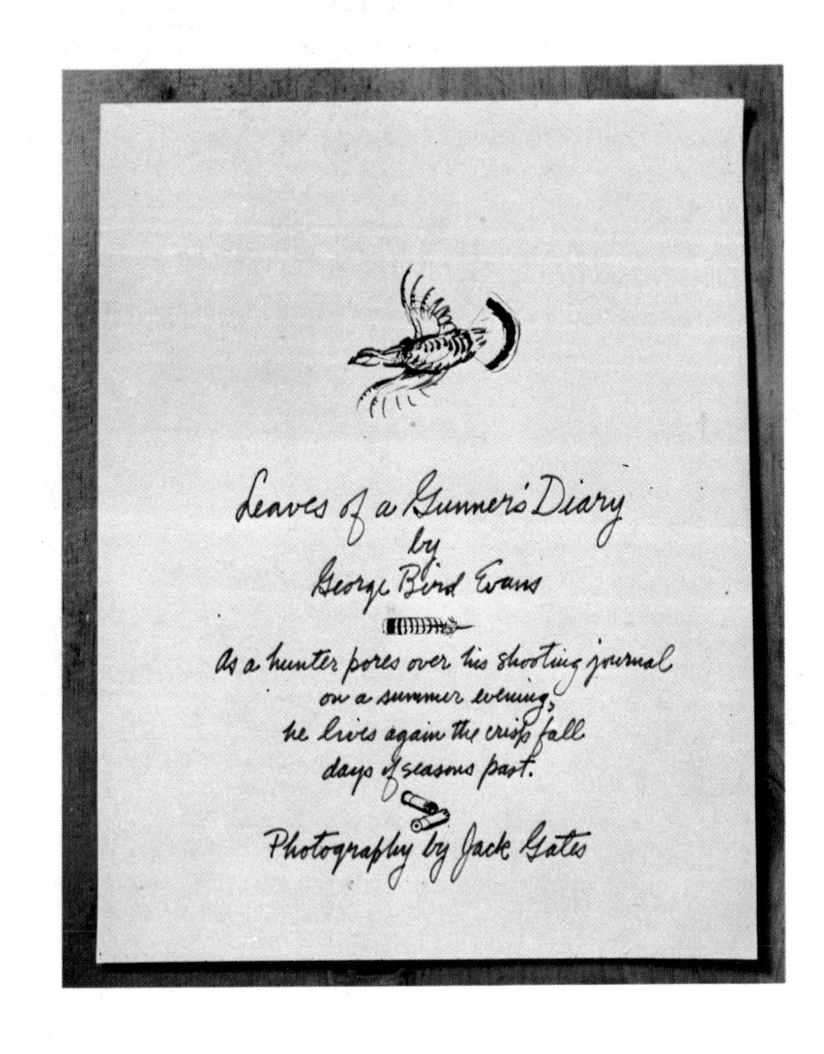
Leaves of a Gunner's Diary
by
George Bird Evans
As a hunter pores over his shooting journal
on a summer evening,
he lives again the crisp fall
days of seasons past.
Photography by Jack Gates

Sport shooting is more than the quarry, no matter how beautiful the piece of game in hand. Shooting is an experience, a high-keyed moment that becomes a memory almost as soon as it has happened. With the passing of the seasons too many of these memories shift out of focus and are lost.

It isn't always easy to recall where you were hunting the day after Thanksgiving, say, eight years ago—or if you did hunt. Was there a good woodcock flight in 1964? You don't forget a gun, but can you say what your shooting averages on pheasants have been for the past ten years, and with which loads? You have no difficulty describing the most outstanding dog you've owned, but do you know how many productive points he made in his puppy year, how many days you hunted together in his lifetime?

Statistics are not the essence of sport, but the making of them is what gunning is about. Conjuring it up, you are in those coverts again with the breeze in your face, the excitement in your mind. In any shooting—big-game, wildfowl, upland-game—a gun diary is your shooting past where ink, though faded, brings back details as magically as a forgotten fragrance. The keen pleasures of recollection can be summoned by scanning the pages on a warm summer night when it seems the aspens will never turn gold again—then you know they will turn and you will shoot again and afterwards sit by the fire and save it all by writing it down.

A shooting diary may seem something to discover between musty tooled leather, or in an ancient ledger with pale brown entries made when there was leisure to savor a day in coverts enough to want to preserve it. But there are still men who cherish a gun beyond the gun itself because it was handed on to them; men who keep a feather or a wishbone from each bird a certain dog retrieved, or keep that dog's bell or collar

CONTINUED ON PAGE 107

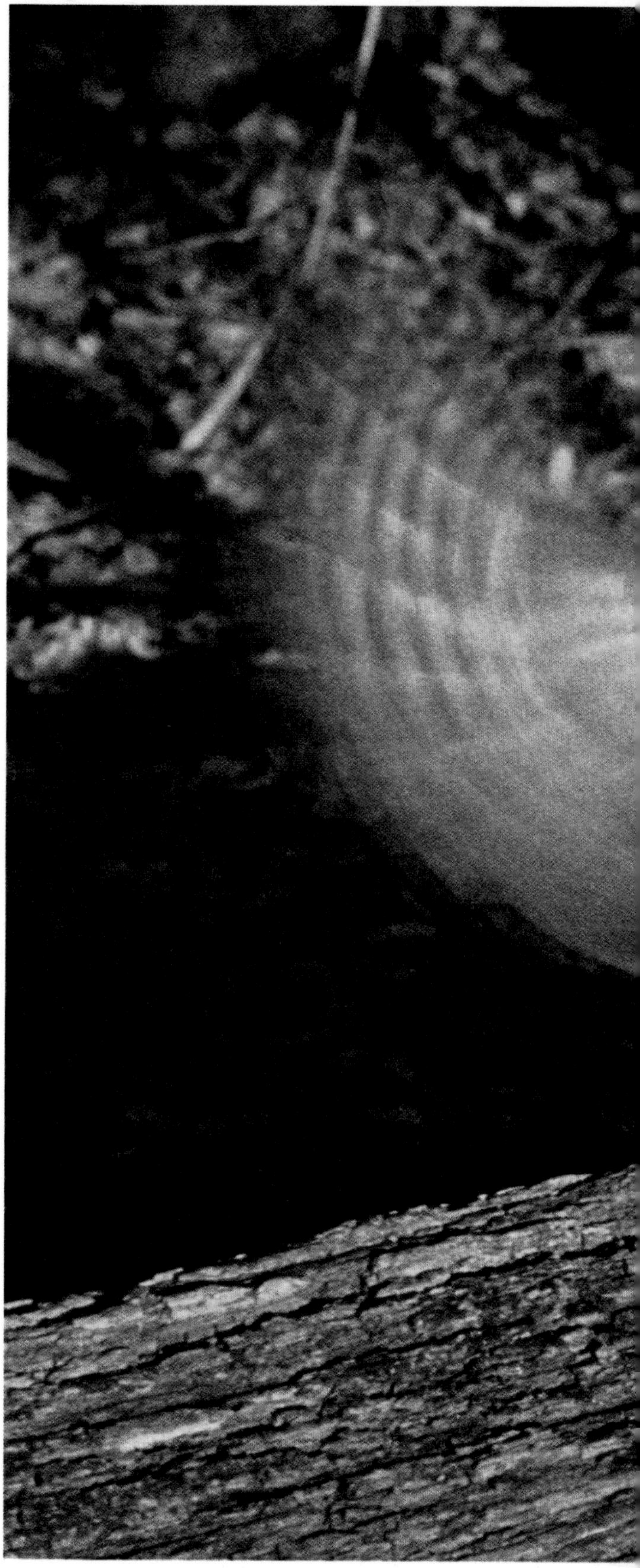

Title pages: On fall evening after hunt, author's desk is laden with guns and woodcock to be mentioned in diary. Above: Drumming on log in classic manner, grouse beats wings incredibly fast.

Just beyond the bonefish shallows lie game-rich depths where wahoo compete with other savage battlers and there is no predicting what will strike next.

BERMUDA: CORAL BANKS AND BIG FISH

by Ellington White

photography by Marvin E. Newman

Title pages: Big wahoo lunges furiously in last run. Left: Same fish is finally gaffed and boated. Below: Close-up views show unusual jaw structure and mackerel-like fins and tail.

Some years ago while living in Bermuda I spent a lot of time bonefishing in the bright shallows that hug the island's western end. On that island fishing seemed as natural as going to the post office. I filled my pockets with weighted bucktails, climbed aboard my motor bike—my rod braced across the handle bars—and set off down the Middle Road in the direction of Somerset. One place in particular appealed to me. This was Whitney Bay, usually referred to locally as Whale Bay: a few acres of dazzling white sand covered by water so clear it might have come from the sky only that morning. I never caught many bonefish at Whale Bay. In open water such as that, the slightest movement I made must have registered on a fish with the impact of an earthquake. But it was an exhilarating experience nevertheless. More often than not I had the place all to myself. Long-tailed tropic

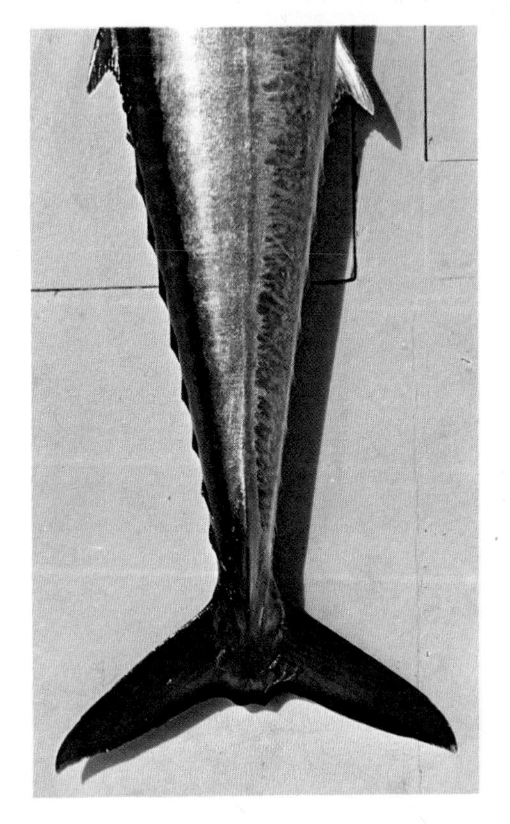

Below: Perching on high rocks, angler scans Whale Bay for bonefish schools. Bottom: Bonefish streaks through shallows after striking fly. Right: Author's skiff works along productive flats.

birds would come down from the nests in the cliffs to see what I was doing; and bonefish, when they did arrive, appeared as shadows sliding across the white sand.

Since then I have bonefished in other parts of the world, from Florida to Mexico, but never have I felt as close to the heart of fishing as I felt at Whale Bay, so close that any other form of fishing (any other form of human activity, really) seemed to me trivial in comparison.

One of the unique delights of Bermuda bonefishing, owing to the volcanic origins of the island, is that one has at his disposal a built-in "tuna tower" from which he can observe the flats. I am talking about the cliffs found along most of the shoreline. Whale Bay is a case in point; here the sea makes a small dent in the island, and from the cliffs overlooking it one is able to take in the

CONTINUED ON PAGE 114

No small arm had ever been so accurate, so efficient f

The Jaeger: a rifled wonder

by Harold L. Peterson / photography by J. Barry O'R

unting, target shooting, even warfare.

Preceding pages (from top): Magnificent German jaeger by I. G. Horneffer, c. 1735; carved-horn powder flask of late 18th century; rare double-barreled jaeger made by A. Huhnstock of Hanover, c. 1775; and ivory-gripped Austrian hunting sword of same period. Right, top: Relief carving and inlays of staghorn, ivory, and bone on stock of Horneffer rifle. Bottom: Engraving, chiseling, and gold inlays on lock of same rifle.

The claim of perfection would appear absurd in connection with rifles built more than two-and-a-half centuries ago, when gun design was still relatively primitive. For its time, nevertheless, one type of rifle—the jaeger—represented a new peak of perfection. Many students consider it the first really important rifle in history. Even those who would dispute this claim grant that the jaeger was undoubtedly one of the world's great guns. A marvel of accuracy and efficiency, it not only earned acclaim as a hunting and target arm, but was issued by military leaders to specially trained marksmen.

Its name was derived from the German word *Jäger*—meaning a hunter or a gamekeeper, a marksman or a sportsman of some sort, even a military rifleman. A German would certainly not use the word to refer to his firearm. English-speaking people, however, adopted the term to designate a fine short rifle that originated in central Europe and was used throughout much of the civilized world.

Like many another great gun before and after, the jaeger was the product of a long evolutionary process. It began, perhaps with the invention of rifling in the very same area of Europe, among the same sort of men who eventually produced the jaeger. No one knows who the inventor of rifling was. Several names have been suggested, but there is not one iota of proof. Even the exact date is lost. Italian scholars of a century ago cited an inventory of 1476 with an entry that they interpreted as meaning rifles, but modern students feel that this is probably a mistranslation. Another early historian mentions an invitation to a shooting match at Leipzig in 1498, which purportedly distinguished between events for smoothbores and rifles, but no scholar of this century has been able to find this invitation.

Both of these dates are possible, if unprovable. Definite evidence, however, comes from an object rather than a document. This is a rifle made for the famous Hapsburg ruler who later became Maximilian I of the Holy Roman Empire. On its stock it bears the arms used by Maximilian after he became king of Germany in 1493 and before he became Holy Roman Emperor in 1508. Thus, it is almost precisely datable. And it is a true rifle, with a bronze barrel rifled with multiple grooves in a slow twist and equipped with a peep sight for accurate long-range shooting. Originally this was a snapping matchlock, but the lock has been lost ever since the first picture of the gun appeared in the work of the British antiquarian Sir Samuel Rush Meyrick in 1830.

The function of the twisting rifling grooves was, of course, to make the bullet spin as it left the barrel and sped towards its mark. Spinning balls traveled straighter and hit harder. No one understood why they did, but the results were obvious to all. Theoreticians argued that the devil must be involved, either because he could not ride a spinning ball and lead it astray, or because

Top left: Muzzle view of .60-caliber Huhnstock and .58-caliber Horneffer jaegers shows bead front sights and multigroove rifling. Top right: Brass-mounted Huhnstock double rifle, originally one of a set, employs V-notch rear sight. Bottom: Jaeger made by celebrated Bavarian gunsmith, Johann Andre Kuchenreuter, c. 1775. His barrels were so famous for accuracy that they were used by makers as far away as England.

he could ride it and guide it towards its devilish end. Actually, the spin of the ball sets up a gyroscopic action that minimizes the tendency of a ball to drift under the influence of differences in densities within the ball and surface irregularities without. It was centuries before ballistics experts arrived at this conclusion, however. Early riflemakers probably got their inspiration from the spin of arrows.

Another cause of the rifle's greater accuracy lay in the tight fit of the bullet. In smoothbores, the balls fit loosely to speed loading and minimize the effects of powder fouling. In a rifle a loose-fitting ball is ineffective since it will not take the spin the grooves were designed to impart. The first rifle shooters soon discovered the importance of a tight fit. The obvious way to obtain this was to make the ball a little bigger than the bore and force it into the grooves by sheer strength. This was hard on ramrods, and it also produced tired arms that often shook and hampered aiming. Furthermore, it was very, very slow. Within a few years some genius discovered that wrapping the bullet in a greased patch of cloth or thin leather would produce the same result—and it was a lot easier on arms and ramrods. Also, it helped soften and wipe out the powder fouling which had made frequent cleanings necessary when tight-fitting balls were used. It was even a little faster. Riflemen probably began to use such patched balls during the 1500's. Actual patches survive from about 1600 in Dresden, Germany. And as far away as Spain, Alonzo Martínez de Espinar described the use of patched balls as standard practice in his *Treatise on Guns and Shooting* of 1644. Some shooters, however, continued to drive outsized balls down the barrels of their rifles as late as 1800.

No matter how the rifleman obtained his tight fit, it meant that the bullet left the muzzle in a precise direction. In the smoothbores the loose-fitting balls literally bounced down the bore, and they could take off at any one of a number of angles depending upon the last bounce. The bounce of the ball was eliminated as a factor in the rifle so the shooter could at least be sure that his bullet departed in the direction he aimed.

With the possibility of real accuracy in his grasp, the scientific shooter soon began to try to eliminate other variables. He practiced with his rifle until he understood all its idiosyncrasies. He learned what charges of powder combined with the weight of his bullet to produce the best results at given ranges. Since the strength of powder varied considerably in those early days, he became a devotee of the powder tester, a device with which he could measure the effectiveness of each new batch he purchased and alter his loads accordingly. He also acquired powder measures to insure accurate charges. Maximilian's rifle has such a measure hollowed in the end of its ramrod, but other marksmen found them handy in combination with their powder flasks, or with the spanners for

CONTINUED ON PAGE 118

Da reit Tessilo an der gayt
ain herr von Bayren

Masterpieces of the Chase and the Catch

The universally practiced arts of hunting game and catching fish have fascinated painters in every time and place. But perhaps most interesting to modern sportsmen are pictures containing clues to the manner in which these enterprises were conducted in centuries past. On these and the following pages is an array of fine art ranging over 2,000 years in time and vividly revealing the effective but now-vanished techniques and equipment employed. All that persists unchanged is the patience and determination expressed by the faces of hunters and fishermen.

Preceding pages: Mounted hunters (left) are pursuing boar or stag. Medieval German crossbow has long trigger, twisted hemp or flax string. Italian wildfowling scene of same period depicts both crossbow and long bow accurate enough to hit sitting birds with harpoons and long arrows. Above: 18th-century Genoese anglers use long, supple rods to still-fish shallows of bay; lines seem to be weighted. Far left: In self-portrait, Paolo

Preceding pages: Lucas Cranach (1472-1553) painted stags being driven into river, where noblemen ambushed them; powerful crossbows had mechanical device to draw string. Above: Well-placed first arrow of ancient Roman hunter may have been intended as instructive. Top right: Pietro Longhi painted popular 18th-century Venetian amusements, which included bow-hunting for ducks. Bottom right: Jost Sustermans painting illustrates old practice of hanging wild ducks to improve delicacy of flesh.

MYSTERIES OF THE LOADING BENCH

Perfection in any sport may be an illusion, but to the handloading marksman the goal is worthy of an endless search.

by Major George C. Nonte, Jr.

photography by Arie deZanger

Preceding pages: One of John Buhmiller's .450 Magnum wildcat rifles rests on loading bench with dies, Bonanza loading press, and cartridges handloaded with special bullets for elephants and Cape buffalo. Right: Remington .22/250 varmint rifle with Redfield 16X scope stands next to cartridges, 55-grain Sierra bullets, and Bushnell 20X spotting scope. Small black device in front of tripod is Pacific portable loading tool.

There was nothing to use as a shooting rest, but my hunting companion had his left hand braced against a mesquite while he steadied his rifle and took aim at a plump Texas whitetail not much over a hundred yards away. "Steady as a bench," he whispered, then held his breath and began the squeeze. It would have been an easy shot with his scoped 6mm bolt-action—except that the buck was facing him, standing in a thicket, and almost entirely screened by impenetrable foliage. Only a small patch of brisket showed, and this had to be the hunter's target if he wished to make a swift, one-shot kill. Nevertheless, I felt no surprise when the deer dropped. I had watched this man shoot before.

What did surprise me was his reaction when he examined his trophy. He was happy enough about the rack, happier still about the obviously prime venison, but he was displeased that the bullet had entered a trifle higher than he had intended. He was reasonably sure the cause was not in his aim but in the cartridge. The ammunition he was using, he explained, was shooting a bit high, and he felt he should have sighted in his rifle a little lower or else taken the time to make up a new batch of loads. For him, even a "perfect" one-shot kill was not perfect enough.

In terms of hunting and fishing skills, excellence—even perfection—is a relative concept rather than an absolute, except perhaps theoretically. The ultimate goal is elusive, mysterious, even unattainable. This is why larger antlers, heavier game fish on lighter tackle, smaller one-hole target groups continue year after year to break old records. The essence of the sport lies at least as much in the quest as in the achievement.

For me as for more and more serious riflemen in this era of constantly improved equipment, a large part of the quest takes the form of an incurable but splendid obsession with handloading. The search for a "perfect" cartridge, usually to be employed in only one rifle for only one type of shooting, is marked by the spoor of rules and data as well as by the frustrations known as variables. In many ways it parallels the chase itself. On summer days or winter nights it can be a welcome sublimation of the atavistic hunting desire. There are those who claim that they reload cartridges in order to save money on certain expensive types of ammunition, but shortly after making such statements (for the benefit of wife or conscience) they are likely to spend large sums on the latest loading gear.

Little is said or written about the real motive, perhaps for fear of seeming overly romantic, but the key has to be the yearning for a mysterious, almost mystical perfection. To the uninitiated this may be puzzling in view of the fact that superb ready-made sporting ammunition can be had today in an almost unbelievable variety of types, calibers, and loadings. Accuracy and performance acceptable for almost any normal use

CONTINUED ON PAGE 122

WINCHESTER
PRECISION "SIGHTING-IN"
CORRECTION CHART
HOW TO USE THE CHART
IMPORTANT—Your rifle should be shot from a well padded rest, under calm wind conditions, resting forearm, not barrel, on pad.

Knickerbockered salmon angler exemplifies British influence on American fishermen of Van Dyke's era.

Fisherman's Luck
by
Henry Van Dyke

Two stories from the pen of a fondly remembered American angling writer.

Many anglers still recall with affection their boyhood reading of Henry Van Dyke, whose works influenced the attitudes of American fishermen from the 1880's until well into the twentieth century. It was common during that era to emulate the English in a number of respects—from the wearing of knickerbockers and tweeds to the preference for casting only to the rise. Van Dyke embraced some of the English customs, but he also advocated American fly patterns and the American style of fast-water trout fishing. And the split-bamboo rod he favored was of a type introduced in 1848 by Samuel Phillippe, a Pennsylvanian.

The son of a prominent Presbyterian churchman, Henry Van Dyke was born in 1852. Successfully pursuing several careers, he became a well-known clergyman, writer, university professor, and U.S. Minister to the Netherlands and Luxembourg, yet somehow he found time to become one of this country's foremost fly fishermen.

His writings about fishing are characterized by lyrical descriptions, wit, and philosophical reflections. He avoided taking a didactic tone by offering angling advice in the form of narratives about his own experiences. This approach is exemplified in the two passages presented here. The first, a rambling account entitled "The Ristigouche from a Horse-Yacht," was written in 1888, and included in an 1895 Van Dyke book called Little Rivers. *"The Thrilling Moment" appeared four years later in a volume entitled* Fisherman's Luck.

THE RISTIGOUCHE FROM A HORSE-YACHT

The boundary line between the Province of Quebec and New Brunswick, for a considerable part of its course, resembles the name of the poet Keats; it is "writ in water." But like his fame, it is water that never fails, —the limpid current of the river Ristigouche.

The railway crawls over it on a long bridge at Metapedia, and you are dropped in the darkness somewhere between midnight and dawn. When you open your window-shutters the next morning, you see that the village is a disconsolate hamlet, scattered along the track as if it had been shaken by chance from an open freight-car. . . . Here it was that I found my friend Favonius . . . ingenuously arrayed in gray knickerbockers, a flannel shirt, and a soft hat, waiting to take me on his horse-yacht.

Have you ever seen a horse-yacht? Sometimes it is called a scow; but that sounds common. Sometimes it is called a house-boat; but that is too English. What does it profit a man to have a whole dictionary full of language at his service, unless he can invent a new and suggestive name for his friend's pleasure-craft? The foundation of the horse-yacht—if a thing that floats may be called fundamental—is a flat-bottomed boat, some fifty feet long and ten feet wide, with a draft of about eight inches. The deck is open for fifteen feet aft of the place where the bowsprit ought to be; behind that it is completely covered by a house, cabin, cottage, or whatever you choose to call it, with straight sides and a peaked roof of a very early Gothic pattern. Looking in at the door you see, first of all, two cots, one on either side of the passage; then an open space with a dining-table, a stove, and some chairs; beyond that a pantry with shelves, and a great chest for provisions. A door at the back opens into the kitchen, and from that another door opens into a sleeping-room for the boatmen. A huge wooden tiller curves over the stern of the boat, and the helmsman stands upon the kitchen-roof. Two canoes are floating behind, holding back, at the end of their long tow-ropes, as if reluctant to follow so clumsy a leader.

While we were stowing away our trunks and bags under the cots, and making an equitable division of the hooks upon the walls, the motive power of the yacht stood patiently upon the shore, stamping a hoof, now and then, or shaking a shaggy head in mild protest against the flies. Three more pessimistic-looking horses I never saw. They were harnessed abreast, and fastened by a prodigious tow-rope to a short post in the middle of the forward deck. Their driver was a truculent, brigandish, bearded old fellow in long boots, a blue flannel shirt, and a black sombrero.

Well, as I have said, we were haggling courteously over those hooks in the cabin, when the boat gave a lurch. The bow swung out into the stream. There was a scrambling and clattering of iron horse-shoes on the rough shingle of the bank; and when we looked out of doors, our house was moving.

The Ristigouche is a noble stream, stately and swift and strong. It rises among the dense forests in the northern part of New Brunswick—a moist upland region, of never-failing springs and innumerous lakes—and pours a flood of clear, cold water one hundred and fifty miles northward and eastward through the hills into the Bay of Chaleurs.

As soon as one learns to regard the horse-yacht as a sort of moving house, it appears admirable. There is no dust or smoke, no rumble of wheels, or shriek of whistles. You are gliding along steadily through an ever-green world; skirting the silent hills; passing from one side of the river to the other when the horses have to swim the current

Sketched on Long Island waters where Van Dyke sometimes fished, anglers celebrate opening of trout season, March 15, 1877.

to find a good foothold on the bank. . . . It was possible to stand upon the forward deck and do a little trout-fishing in motion. By watching your chance, when the corner of a good pool was within easy reach, you could send out a hasty line and cajole a sea-trout from his hiding-place. It is true that the tow-ropes and the post made the back cast a little awkward; and the wind sometimes blew the flies up on the roof of the cabin; but then, with patience and a short line the thing could be done. I remember a pair of good trout that rose together just as we were going through a boiling rapid; and it tried the strength of my split-bamboo rod to bring those fish to the net against the current and the motion of the boat.

At Cross Point, where the river makes a long loop around a narrow mountain, thin as a saw and crowned on its jagged edge by a rude wooden cross, we stopped for an hour to try the fishing. It was here that I hooked two mysterious creatures, each of which took the fly when it was below the surface, pulled for a few moments in a sullen way and then apparently melted into nothingness. It will always be a source of regret to me that the nature of these fish must remain unknown. While they were on the line it was the general opinion that they were heavy trout; but no sooner had they departed, than I became firmly convinced, in accordance with a psychological law which holds good all over the world, that they were both enormous salmon.

The Slide Pool is in the wildest and most picturesque part of the river, about thirty-five miles above Metapedia. The stream, flowing swiftly down a stretch of rapids between forest-clad hills, runs straight toward the base of an eminence so precipitous that the trees can hardly find a foothold upon it, and seem to be climbing up in haste on either side of the long slide which leads to the summit. The current, barred by the wall of rock, takes a great sweep to the right, dashing up at first in angry waves, then falling away in oily curves and eddies, until at last it sleeps in a black deep, apparently almost motionless, at the foot of the hill. It was here, on the upper edge of the stream, opposite to the slide, that we brought our floating camp to anchor for some days. What does one do in such a watering-place?

Let us take a "specimen day." It is early morning, or to be more precise, about eight of the clock, and the white fog is just beginning to curl and drift away from the surface of the river. Sooner than this it would be idle to go out. The preternaturally early bird in his greedy haste may catch the worm; but the salmon never take the fly until the fog has lifted; and in this the scientific angler sees, with gratitude, a remarkable adaptation of the laws of nature to the tastes of man. The canoes are waiting at the front door. We step into them and push off, Favonius going up the stream a couple of miles to the mouth of the Patapedia, and I down, a little shorter distance, to the famous Indian House Pool. The slim boat glides easily on the current, with a smooth buoyant motion, quickened by the strokes of the paddles in the bow and the stern. We pass around two curves in the river and find ourselves at the head of the pool. Here the man in the stern drops the anchor, just on the edge of the bar where the rapid breaks over into the deeper water. The long rod is lifted; the fly unhooked from the reel; a few feet of line pulled through the rings.

First cast,—to the right, straight across the stream, about twenty feet: the current carries the fly down with a semicircular sweep, until it comes in line with the bow of the canoe. Second cast,—to the left, straight across the stream, with the same motion: the semicircle is completed, and the fly hangs quivering for a few seconds at the lowest point of the arc. Three or four feet of line are drawn from the reel. Third cast to the right; fourth cast to the left. Then a little more line. And so, with widening half-circles, the water is covered, gradually and very carefully, until at length the angler has as much line out as his two-handed rod can lift and swing. Then the first "drop" is finished; the man in the stern quietly pulls up the anchor and lets the boat drift down a few yards; the same process is repeated on the second drop; and so on, until the end of the run is reached and the fly has passed over all the good water. This seems like a very regular and somewhat mechanical proceeding as one describes it, but in the performance it is rendered intensely interesting by the knowledge that at any moment it is liable to be interrupted.

This morning the interruption comes early. At the first cast of the second drop, before the fly has fairly lit, a great flash of silver darts from the waves close by the boat. Usually a salmon takes the fly rather slowly, carrying it under water before he seizes it in his mouth. But this one is in no mood for deliberation. He has hooked himself with a rush, and the line goes whirring madly from the reel as he races down the pool. Keep the point of the rod low; he must have his own way now. Up with the anchor quickly, and send the canoe after him, bowman and sternman paddling with swift strokes. He has reached the deepest water; he stops to think what has happened to him; we have passed around and below him; and now, with the current to help us, we can begin to reel in. Lift the point of the rod, with a strong, steady pull. Put the force of both arms into it. The tough wood will stand the strain. The fish must be moved; he must come to the boat if he is ever to be landed. He gives a little and yields slowly to the pressure. Then suddenly he gives too much, and runs straight toward us. Reel in now as swiftly as possible, or else he will get a slack on the line and escape. Now he stops, shakes his head from side to side, and darts away again across the pool, leaping high out of water. Don't touch the reel! Drop the point of the rod quickly, for if he falls on the leader he will surely break it. Another leap, and another! Truly he is "a merry one," and it will go hard with us to hold him. But those great leaps have exhausted his strength, and now he follows the rod more easily. The men push the boat back to the shallow side of the pool until it touches lightly on the shore. The fish comes slowly in, fighting a little and making a few short runs; he is tired and turns slightly on his side; but even yet he is a heavy weight on the line, and it seems a wonder that so slight a thing as the leader can guide and draw him. Now he is close to the boat. The boatman steps out on a rock with his gaff. Steadily now and slowly, lift the rod, bending it backward. A sure stroke of the steel! a great splash! and the salmon is lifted upon the shore. How he flounces about on the stones. Give him the *coup de grace* at once, for his own sake as well as for ours. And now look at him, as he lies there on the green leaves. Broad back; small head tapering to a point; clean, shining sides with a few black spots on them; it is a fish fresh-run from the sea, in perfect condition, and that is the reason why he has given such good sport.

We must try for another before we go back. Again fortune favours us, and at eleven o'clock we pole up the river to the camp with two good salmon in the canoe. Hardly have we laid them away in the ice-box, when Favonius comes dropping down from Patapedia with three fish, one of them a twenty-four pounder.

There were some days, however, when our benevolent intentions toward the salmon were frustrated; mornings when they refused to rise, and evenings when they escaped even the skilful endeavours of Favonius. In vain did he try every fly in his book, from the smallest "Silver Doctor" to the largest "Golden Eagle." The "Black Dose" would not move them. The "Durham Ranger" covered the pool in vain. On days like this, if a stray fish rose, it was hard to land him, for he was usually but slightly hooked.

I remember one of these shy creatures which led me a pretty dance at the mouth of Patapedia. He came to the fly just at dusk, rising very softly and quietly, as if he did not really care for it but only wanted to see what it was like. He went down at once into deep water, and began the most dangerous and exasperating of all salmon-tactics, moving around in slow circles and shaking his head from side to side, with sullen pertinacity. This is called "jigging," and unless it can be stopped, the result is fatal.

I could not stop it. That salmon was determined to jig. He knew more than I did.

The canoe followed him down the pool. He jigged away past all three of the inlets of the Patapedia, and at last, in the still, deep water below, after we had laboured with him for half an hour, and brought him near enough to see that he was immense, he calmly opened his mouth and the fly came back to me void. That was a sad evening, in which all the consolations of philosophy were needed.

At last the days of idleness were ended. We took down the long rods, put away the heavy reels, made the canoes fast to the side of the house, embarked the three horses on the front deck, and then dropped down with the current, swinging along through the rapids, and drifting slowly through the still places, now grounding on a hidden rock, and now sweeping around a sharp curve, until at length we saw the roofs of Metapedia and the ugly bridge of the railway spanning the river. There we left our floating house . . . like some strange relic of the flood, stranded on the shore. And as we climbed the bank we looked back and wondered whether Noah was sorry when he said good-bye to his ark.

THE THRILLING MOMENT

Every moment of life, I suppose, is more or less of a turning-point. Opportunities are swarming around us all the time, thicker than gnats at sundown. We walk through a cloud of chances, and if we were always conscious of them they would worry us almost to death.

But happily our sense of uncertainty is soothed and cushioned by habit, so that we can live comfortably with it. Only now and then, by way of special excitement, it starts up wide awake. We perceive how delicately our fortune is poised and balanced on the pivot of a single incident.

The meditative angler is not exempt from these sensational periods. There are times when all the uncertainty of his chosen pursuit seems to condense itself into one big chance, and stand out before him like a salmon on the top wave of a rapid. He sees that his luck hangs by a single strand, and he cannot tell whether it will hold or break. This is his thrilling moment, and he never forgets it.

Mine came to me in the autumn of 1894, on the banks of the Unpronounceable River, in the Province of Quebec. It was the last day of the open season for ouananiche, and we had set our hearts on catching some good fish to take home with us. We walked up from the mouth of the river, four preposterously long and rough miles, to the famous fishing-pool, "*la place de pêche à Boivin.*" It was a noble day for walking; the air was clear and crisp, and all the hills around us were glowing with the crimson foliage of those little bushes which God created to make burned lands look beautiful. The trail ended in a precipitous gully, down which we scrambled with high hopes, only to find that the river was in a condition which made angling absurd if not impossible.

There must have been a cloud-burst among the mountains, for the water was coming down in flood. The stream was bank-full, gurgling and eddying out among the bushes, and rushing over the shoal where the fish used to lie, in a brown torrent ten feet deep. Our last day with the land-locked salmon seemed destined to be a failure, and we must wait eight months before we could have another. There were three of us in the disappointment, and we shared it according to our temperaments.

Paul virtuously resolved not to give up while there was a chance left, and wandered down-stream to look for an eddy where he might pick up a small fish. Ferdinand, our guide, resigned himself without a sigh to the consolation of eating blueberries, which he always did with great cheerfulness. But I, being more cast down than either of my comrades, sought out a convenient seat

among the rocks, and, adapting my anatomy as well as possible to the irregularities of nature's upholstery, pulled from my pocket *An Amateur Angler's Days in Dove Dale*, and settled down to read myself into a Christian frame of mind.

Before beginning, my eyes roved sadly over the pool once more. It was but a casual glance. It lasted only for an instant. But in that fortunate fragment of time I distinctly saw the broad tail of a big ouananiche rise and disappear in the swift water at the very head of the pool.

I said nothing to my companions. It would have been unkind to disturb them with expectations which might never be realized. My immediate duty was to get within casting distance of that salmon.

The way along the shore of the pool was difficult. The bank was very steep, and the rocks by the river's edge were broken and

Guide has found action for fisherman on northeastern lake in 1906 painting by outdoor illustrator H. S. Watson.

glibbery. Presently I came to a sheer wall of stone, perhaps thirty feet high, rising directly from the deep water.

There was a tiny ledge or crevice running part of the way across the face of this wall, and by this four-inch path I edged along, holding my rod in one hand, and clinging affectionately with the other to such clumps of grass and little bushes as I could find. There was one small huckleberry plant to which I had a particular attachment. It was fortunately a firm little bush, and as I held to it I remembered Tennyson's poem which begins "*Flower in the crannied wall*," and reflected that if I should succeed in plucking out this flower, "root and all," it would probably result in an even greater increase of knowledge than the poet contemplated.

The ledge in the rock now came to an end. But below me in the pool there was a sunken reef; and on this reef a long log had caught, with one end sticking out of the water, within jumping distance. It was the only chance. To go back would have been dangerous. An angler with a large family dependent upon him for support has no right to incur unnecessary perils.

Besides, the fish was waiting for me at the upper end of the pool!

So I jumped; landed on the end of the log; felt it settle slowly down; ran along it like a small boy on a seesaw, and leaped off into shallow water just as the log rolled from the ledge.

It went wallowing through the pool and down the rapid like a playful hippopotamus. I watched it with interest and congratulated myself that I was no longer embarked upon it. On that craft a voyage down the Unpronounceable River would have been short.

But now all was well, for I was within reach of the fish. A little scrambling over the rocks brought me to a point where I could easily cast over him. He was lying in a swift, narrow channel between two large stones. It was a snug resting place, and no doubt he would remain there for some time.

I carefully tested a brand-new leader, and attached it to the line with great deliberation. . . . Then I gave my whole mind to the important question of a wise selection of flies.

Now, in regard to flies there are two theories. The old, conservative theory is, that on a bright day you should use a dark, dull fly, because it is less conspicuous. So I followed that theory first and put on a Great Dun and a Dark Montreal. I cast them delicately over the fish, but he would not look at them.

Then I perverted myself to the new, radical theory which says that on a bright day you must use a light, gay fly, because it is more in harmony with the sky, and therefor less noticeable. Accordingly I put on a Professor and a Parmacheene Belle; but this combination of learning and beauty had no attraction for the ouananiche.

Then I fell back on a theory of my own, to the effect that the ouananiche have an aversion to red, and prefer yellow and brown. So I tried various combinations of flies in which these colours predominated.

Then I abandoned all theories and went straight through my book, trying something from every page, and winding up with that lure which the guides consider infallible,—"a Jock o' Scott that cost fifty cents at Quebec." But it was all in vain.

At this psychological moment I heard behind me a voice of hope,—the song of a grasshopper: not one of those fat-legged, green-winged imbeciles that feebly tumble in the summer fields, but a game grasshopper,— one of those thin-shanked, brown-winged fellows that leap like kangaroos, and fly like birds, and sing *Kri-karee-karee-kri*.

It is not really a song, I know, but it sounds like one; and, if you had heard that Kri-karee carolling as I chased him over the rocks, you would have been sure that he was mocking me.

I believed that he was the predestined lure for that ouananiche; but it was hard to persuade him to fulfill his destiny. I slapped at him with my hat, but he was not there. I grasped at him on the bushes, and brought away "nothing but leaves." At last he made his way to the very edge of the water and poised himself on a stone, with his legs well tucked in for a long leap and a bold flight to the other side of the river. It was my final opportunity. I made a desperate grab at it and caught the grasshopper.

My premonition proved to be correct. When that Kri-karee, invisibly attached to my line, went floating down the stream, the ouananiche was surprised. It was the fourteenth of September, and he had supposed the grasshopper season was over. The unexpected temptation was too strong for him. He rose with a rush. . . . I was fast to the best land-locked salmon of the year.

But the situation was not without its embarrassments. My rod weighed only four and a quarter ounces; the fish weighed between six and seven pounds. The water was furious and headstrong. I had only thirty yards of line and no landing-net.

"Holà! Ferdinand!" I cried. *"Apporte la nette, vite! A beauty! Hurry up!"*

I thought it must be an hour while he was making his way over the hill, through the underbrush, around the cliff. Again and again the fish ran out my line almost to the last turn. A dozen times he leaped from the water, shaking his silvery sides. Twice he tried to cut the leader across a sunken ledge. But at last he was played out, and came in quietly towards the point of the rock. At the same moment Ferdinand appeared.

Now, the use of the net is really the most difficult part of angling. And Ferdinand is the best netsman in the Lake St. John country. He never makes the mistake of trying to scoop a fish in motion. He does not grope around with aimless, futile strokes as if he were feeling for something in the dark. He does not entangle the dropper-fly in the net and tear the tail-fly out of the fish's mouth.

He quietly sinks the net in the water, and waits until he can see the fish distinctly, lying perfectly still and within reach. Then he makes a swift movement, like that of a mower swinging the scythe, takes the fish into the net head-first, and lands him.

I felt sure that Ferdinand was going to do the trick in precisely this way with my ouananiche. Just at the right instant he made one quick, steady swing of the arms, and—the head of the net broke clean off . . . and went floating away with the fish in it!

All seemed to be lost. But Ferdinand was equal to the occasion. He seized a long, crooked stick that lay in a pile of driftwood on the shore, sprang into the water up to his waist, caught the net as it drifted past, and dragged it to land, with the ultimate ouananiche, the prize of the season, still glittering through its meshes.

This is the story of my most thrilling moment as an angler.

But which was the moment of the deepest thrill?

Was it when the huckleberry bush saved me from a watery grave, or when the log rolled under my feet and started down the river? Was it when the fish rose, or when the net broke, or when the long stick captured it?

No, it was none of these. It was when the Kri-karee sat with his legs tucked under him on the brink of the stream. That was the turning-point. The fortunes of the day depended on the comparative quickness of the reflex action of his neural ganglia and mine. That was the thrilling moment.

I see it now. A crisis is really the commonest thing in the world. The reason why life sometimes seems dull to us is because we do not perceive the importance and the excitement of getting bait. ◎

Central states. Both the fish and the fishing caught the nation's fancy. In an era that honored sportsmen, the bass became America's favorite aquatic game, recognized as "inch for inch and pound for pound the gamest fish that swims."

I was introduced to this rapidly expanding sport as a boy of twelve. Born and raised in Alaska, I was precociously and deeply involved with flies and fly fishing. Then our family spent the summer of 1917 at Round Lake, New York, where largemouth bass were well-established. In nearby Saratoga Lake, both largemouths and smallmouths had become quite plentiful.

In the village fountain-pool at Round Lake, for all to see, there swam a seven-and-a-half pound largemouth recently transferred from Round Lake itself, with a school of golden shiners for company. On the July day of our arrival, the town fathers released a barnyard duck and six fluffy yellow ducklings in the pool to give additional interest. The following day there were only five ducklings—and considerable argument as to whether a bass could possibly swallow a duckling, or whether a mink or some other predator should be blamed. Two days later the nonbelievers were convinced when a pair of spinsters paused to throw bread crumbs to the ducklings and saw one of them engulfed by the bass.

I suppose it may have been incidents like this that led to some of the later experimentation with artificial bass lures which looked like creatures other than minnows. It was found possible to attract bass with lures that (more or less) resembled frogs, mice, eels, worms, and crawfish. There have even been some fairly successful concoctions that looked like no live bait at all, but simply used a wobbling, popping, or darting action, or a shine or bright colors that aroused the attacking instincts of a bass.

My father borrowed or rented for me a hard-used but still usable casting reel, a stiff bait-casting rod five feet long (with the advent of artificial lures, bait-casting rods had become shorter), and a single minnow-like plug of the wobbling type. The erstwhile owner had called this plug a "dowell jack." It was red and white—colors which fishermen of that day associated with Christmas candies but surely not with bass baits. That summer, far from Alaska's cold water and big trout, was important to me for two reasons: I learned to swim and I fell in love with bass fishing.

New developments in bait casting were coming along rapidly. During the winters I read catalogs; in the springs I spent all my Christmas money and savings on tackle, and in the summers, wherever in the Northeast we spent them, I fished primarily for bass. The second season I had an outfit of my own: a Meisselbach reel, an Abbey & Imbrie rod, a Kingfisher line, and a small assortment of plugs. I still had the Dowagiac wobbler and I had also bought a Decker, a surface plug with a revolving head; a Tango, a big plug that swam backward like a crawfish and ran deep; and a long, slim, cigar-like sinking plug, with propellers at each end, called a Panatella. In addition, I had carved out of cedar (the recommended wood) half a dozen plugs that copied such favorites as the Bass-Oreno, plus one or two relatively unsuccessful inventions of my own. In looking back to that summer I can remember no magnificent catches, only a great northern pike in the Hudson that hit my plug and threw it high into the sky.

By 1919 the first anti-backlash reel had been brought out by South Bend. Basically, an anti-backlash device is an internal dragging mechanism which gradually slows down the spool in proportion to the loss of speed by the lure. The lure and line move fastest at the beginning of the cast, when energy is imparted to them by the whip of

During backcast, weight of lure acutely bends springy tip section of good bait-casting rod, adding whip action when lure is propelled forward.

the rod. Without some sort of drag, the reel will not lose its momentum as quickly as the lure loses its speed, so there is a tendency for it to overrun the line and thereby cause a backlash.

The anti-backlash drag simply keeps the spool from turning faster than line is unwound and thereby prevents snarling. This feature and the level wind were to make bait casting moderately easy to learn. Until then, bait casting demanded an educated thumb to keep the spool from overrunning during the cast. A bad backlash could take half an hour or more to clear up. The level-wind mechanism is an attachment which moves back and forth horizontally to spread the line evenly on the spool during the retrieve. This, too, greatly reduces the possibility of a backlash. The level wind was introduced by the Wisconsin firm of Wheeler & McGregor, and today's versions still embody the original design.

By thumbing the spool during the cast, the angler can manually slow the rotation just enough to keep lure and reel in time. Perfect thumbing accomplishes this even better than anti-backlash devices. The novice can simply set the anti-backlash drag a little harder than normal and prevent all backlashes, but this will shorten his casts because of the extra drag. For best casting, anyone but the expert should set the spool tension of the anti-backlash device so that when the rod is held horizontally, with the lure reeled up to the tip and the reel put in free spool, the lure will descend slowly without need for thumbing. If the drag is lighter and the lure drops quickly, the angler will have to thumb it when casting, and if there is no drag at all from the anti-backlash device, he will have to rely solely on his thumb. He can then obtain maximum speed and distance but he'll need maximum casting and thumbing skill.

At the same time that reels were being significantly improved, the plug makers were going all out on new colors and finishes. The scale finish had been born, made by spraying paint of one color through a wire screen onto a background of another. And in addition to wooden plugs, manufacturers were offering metal lures, painted or shiny spoon-shaped discs that featured an enticing action when drawn through the water. The father of all wobbling spoons, the Dardevle, was invented by Lou Eppinger, a Michigan fisherman who had started by buying split rings, swivels, and treble hooks in a hardware store and making up a few lures at home; they worked so well that he quickly went into commercial production. Bright glass beads were added to some spoons, and little propellers gave others a fast spinning action. Al Foss was selling pork-rind baits with a wiggling strip that rode behind a spinner, pinned to a weighted body and impaled on a single hook. It was a lure that worked pretty well in weeds, and with a protecting wire over the hook point, it could be made essentially weedless.

That year—1919—sports magazines raged with a controversy as to whether or not treble hooks were sporting. I bought a green and silver scale-finish Bass-Oreno on which I replaced the three trebles with single hooks. One still evening at dusk during the first week of fishing I happened to cast a little too far toward the shore and hung that plug in an overhanging branch. A few seconds later when I shook it free it fell to the water, causing the darnedest commotion made by the biggest bass I'd ever had strike. He mouthed the plug hard and then spit it out with no trouble at all. Then and there I was cured of my allegiance to single hooks on bass plugs. I hoped I'd still qualify as a sportsman. At least I'd given it a try.

In 1920 we moved to California, and on the opening day of bass season, after a night of sleepless anticipation, I was out before

dawn on Murray Lake. I had a new Meisselbach free-spool reel (whose spool could revolve freely on the cast without spinning the crank handle) and a luminous Surf-Oreno, the newest, most revolutionary plug in the catalog. Luminous paint was brand new. It was pure magic to see that glowing lure go out into the blackness and come back to the accompaniment of gurgling surface sounds. It thrilled me greatly. But it didn't excite the bass. They disdained it and only began to hit after daylight when I changed to plugs of conventional colors. Moreover, before the season was over I learned that all-black plugs were deadly for bass on the darkest night, a fact which still puzzles me.

So it went. We who were America's most dedicated fishermen fished for everything with all kinds of tackle, but the heart of our fishing was bait casting and bass. Day or night, lake or river, wherever the bass fishing was best, we sought it out. Well into the Thirties the fishing was magnificent. In the summer of '32 I spent many a night from dusk to dawn on Rye Lake or Kensico Reservoir, twenty-five miles from downtown New York, and it was a rare night that didn't produce at least one four-pound smallmouth. In 1933, in the lakes of Maine's St. Croix River drainage, I discovered that any good caster could catch two or three dozen smallmouths a day that would average close to four pounds. In 1934 there were still plenty of four- and five-pound smallmouths and a lot of mighty big pike in Miller Pond, an Adirondack lake in the Saranac chain. Anywhere to the south, the largemouths were big and abundant. In those days big, fat lures with a lot of splash and wiggle were seemingly irresistible.

Bait casting, expanding its sphere, proved to be a fine, if not the favorite, method of catching muskies, walleyes, pickerel, and northern pike. Under some conditions, big trout began to fall to bait-casting lures, and almost any game fish from catfish to coho gave sport on this tackle. Perhaps the biggest thrills of all for the bait caster now lie in the sea. There is no more spectacular fish than the tarpon and no warier nor more exasperating quarry than the striped bass.

Bait casting changed little when it moved from the lakes and rivers to the surf for the capture of stripers, channel bass, bluefish, and other game fish of the sea. The rods are heavier, the reels for surf-casting are bigger, but the principles are the same. In reality, bait casting knows almost no limits. I've used a pound-and-a-half plastic squid with a trolling rod and a 9/0 reel to cast for and hook many giant bluefin tuna. Somewhat lighter, easier-to-cast lines, lures, and rods make it even more reasonable to cast for such ocean rovers as sailfish, wahoo, and marlin. Experiments show that artificial

VIRGIL F. PRYOR AND ED BODEN

lures work for *any* sight-feeding game fish.

Plastic has become very important in the manufacture of today's lures. The old plugs generally were made of cedar or metal or both; then balsa was introduced, and is still used to give some lures a light, exciting action. But plastic is tougher, easy to shape and color, and inexpensive. In addition to rigid plastic plugs designed either for surface action or deep retrieves, there are now flexible plugs which imitate squid, eels, and so on. Plastic worms, so lifelike that they can fool both bass and anglers, are practically indestructible. They catch bass as few lures ever have. Strangely enough, all-black worms and purple worms tend to be most effective.

Now that there are more anglers and greater fishing pressure, there is less good bass water to fish. And there is competition from spinning and spincasting, two such ridiculously easy methods of fishing that anyone can cast a mile and should find it hard to lose any fish he hooks into. These methods, both of which use the fixed-spool reel principle, have made us a nation of casters. But we are still basically casters for bass; and bait casting is growing in popularity again.

The fixed-spool principle calls for light and therefore weaker lines. With it, lighter lures can be cast farther, and backlashes can be completely eliminated. The anti-reverse mechanism and the adjustable drag have greatly simplified the playing of a fish with a spinning reel. But the best bait-casting reels now also incorporate the anti-reverse and the adjustable drag. The Ambassadeur, for instance, which has a beautiful anti-backlash device in its centrifugal brake, plus a smooth level wind, a star drag, and an anti-reverse, in addition to a free spool for casting ease, is neither cheap nor expensive at about $30 for a lifetime reel.

Bait-casting rods are growing longer again. In the Thirties, the standard length was five or five-and-a-half feet. Today's preferred rod is likely to be between five-and-a-

DAVID B. EISENDRATH, JR.

Far left: Beneath contemporary plugs are antique reels made by Meek, Milam, and Fullilove. Left: Wooden spool of 19th century. Below: Meek model of original type made in 1833.

half and six-and-a-half feet long. Fiberglass has made the difference. It's tougher than bamboo and has its own special liveliness. Lines have also improved. Braided Dacron is soft and smooth—and monofilament lines of plastic are now soft enough and strong enough to work well on revolving spools. They have limited stretch and are not yet as effective for all kinds of fishing, but they're tough and cheap and have the big advantage of near-invisibility in the water.

The techniques of bait casting have changed little in the last half century. Most casters use the level-winding reel, which relieves the necessity of constant finger pressure by the left hand to distribute line evenly whenever it is wound in. The anti-backlash devices give us easy casting, although whenever we try to approach the limits of our own or the tackle's capabilities, we still find the need to thumb. The free spool for casting relieves us of the worry of swiftly turning handles that occasionally used to dust our knuckles. It gives a faster start and longer cast by eliminating the turning of the gears and handle as the lure goes out. In recent years, manufacturers have simply added the star drag and the anti-reverse to a venerable basic design.

Some fly-casting purists like to belittle bait casting, claiming that it neither demands the skill nor provides the elegance—the delicacy, the refinements—of true casting sport. This is simply not so, though the *basics* of bait casting are admittedly very easy to master. The spring of the rod is used to whip out a lure weighing a quarter of an ounce or more, and the best casting stroke for combined accuracy and distance is directly overhead. The caster thus establishes a vertical plane of flight for the lure—aiming it as he snaps the rod tip straight up on the backcast, then down again—and his only problem is distance. By determining the right "feel" for each rod, reel, line, and lure combination, he can determine how far to lift the rod on the backcast and how much power to apply to send the plug any particular distance. By varying the power in every cast and governing the distance by the amount of arc used, the best casters attain extreme accuracy.

The side swing may feel easier than the conventional upward rod movement and will give a smoother cast. It can also give a lower trajectory that will shoot lures farther in below overhanging branches, though accuracy is harder to achieve on long casts. Underhand snap casts and the bow-and-arrow cast—in which the lure is held in the hand, rod flexed toward the target area, and released—will work wonders when there isn't room in back for a normal swing.

The most intriguing, the most satisfying type of bait casting is to be found when the accuracy of the cast and the skill required on the retrieve are both at a maximum. This situation is most likely to occur when fishing near a shoreline where fish tend to lie in the shelter of logs, snags, lily pads, and the like, or when fishing a river where there are pools, pockets, and eddies to be covered which call for a spot landing and a specific speed and course of travel by the lure. Even in open water, where the casts are designed simply to cover a maximum area, there can be a great need for skill on the retrieves. How a lure is manipulated by the angler always determines, to a large extent, how many fish he'll catch. This is particularly true with bass, for it isn't hunger alone but pugnaciousness which often leads these fish to strike. They will frequently hit not because they are hungry, but because they have been teased or angered or titillated into attack by a well-worked lure.

By the manner of their retrieves, some anglers have great success with simple surface lures that incorporate no built-in action devices. They use quick, sharp jerks and pauses to make the plug progress across the surface as if it were alive and in agony. To do this well, they use braided Dacron lines which do not stretch. A stretchy monofilament line would soften the lure's motions and make a perfect retrieve impossible with this type of lure, though the stretch can be an advantage when playing a big fish on light line in open water.

The bait caster who fishes the deep water, where bass and many other fish seem to congregate when they're not feeding and to which they retire when the surface waters cool in the fall, learns to think in terms of the contours of a lake bottom. In his mind's eye, he pictures the lure moseying along about a foot off the bottom, rising up as the slope of the bottom lifts, descending with it when it sinks. This is demanding fishing. It calls for a thorough knowledge of how deep a lure will work at a given speed, as well as a knowledge of the lake's bottom.

The more dramatic surface or near-surface fishing is simpler. The retrieve can be at any reasonable speed with any surface or shallow-diving lure, yet still cover the water properly. On the other hand, a strike on the surface is more exciting than a deep strike. The sound, the splash, the fleeting glimpse of the fish itself, all add an aura of excitement. The angler can see the surface lure, see the effects of his rod twitches and his slow or fast, steady or erratic reeling on the lure's action. Although many fish are caught by anglers who simply cast the lure out and reel it in at a steady pace time after time without variation, more and bigger fish are caught by those who use a varying pace and spend extra time on certain areas.

Bass sometimes can be tormented into

Brace of hefty black bass was taken by combination of pinpoint plug casting and slow, teasing, stop-and-go retrieves.

striking a lure that splashes down in their vicinity and alternates between resting quietly and trembling violently for as much as several minutes. For this kind of fishing the angler must know both the water and his fish. He must concentrate his fishing on the spots where the bass are most likely to be. During a single season, anglers often take fish after fish from the same good resting or feeding place, for when one bass is taken from such a spot it is only a matter of days before another will settle in.

Playing a fish in the weeds is not nearly as exciting as catching one in the open, but the strike, which for the experienced angler is the highlight of the whole operation, is just as exciting there as anywhere else. The old saying that a weedless lure is a fishless lure is not entirely true. Really weedless lures will hook a smaller percentage of striking fish, but when the fish are in the weeds, that's where the action is, and it makes sense to stalk them there.

Bait casting has, in all probability, the widest range in lure size and water coverage of any angling method. Its single weakness is the inability to cast very light lures, because it requires a certain amount of weight in any lure to overcome the inertia of the reel spool and start it rotating rapidly. But with lures weighing over a quarter of an ounce, bait casting is more efficient than any other method. A good bait caster can get more distance than a fixed-spool caster with lures from 3/8 of an ounce on up. The rotating spool puts less wear on the line because it comes off the reel straight to the guides, while on the fixed-spool reel, the bail, or line-releasing device, bends the line about ninety degrees when a retrieve is made or a fish is played. The line wear caused by this square corner and the twisting caused by line coming off the reel against the drag during the fish's runs are considered to be the reasons very large tarpon haven't been caught on spinning gear. A long, hard fight tends to accentuate this wear and twisting which are major factors in failure.

The most successful surf-casters use the bait-casting-type reel. It lets them impart their casting power more fully to the lure. Braided line, which is favored by most bait casters, has little stretch, an aid in setting hooks and working a lure in sharp movements. Although either monofilament or braided line can be used on either type, the extra wear on fixed-spool reels works against braided line, and the stretch and spring of monofilament is not always desirable on revolving-spool reels.

As a fisherman learns to read water and to recognize favored hideouts, his fishing takes on new dimensions and becomes more exciting. He cannot cast to a spot where he has hooked or caught a big fish before without a quickening of his pulse. He learns that bass lie under shady branches that overhang deep shorelines, in under the shadows of logs and other sunken obstructions, and in deep pockets of open water extending into patches of lily pads. He cannot see a place that seems ideal for a fish to lie in without excitement. He approaches it with freshening hope, takes extra care to make a cast that will put his lure close to the suspected fish without frightening him, and plans his retrieve to be as tantalizing as he can make it. Some spots he'll consider worth half a dozen casts or more; others he'll gloss over with a single cast and a quick retrieve.

There's great satisfaction in plunking a plug dead center in an open pocket amidst the lily pads, or splashing water up onto a log without touching the wood itself when you think a big bass may be hiding below. Even if no strike follows, there's pleasure in knowing that your eye was sharp, your arm was good, your cast was true. When such casts are consistent, catching fish becomes a kind of a bonus. ◉

Campfire Cookery

Any outdoor dinner, from summer's delicate trout fillets to fall's hearty game pies, can be improved by a dollop of advance planning, a dash of improvisation, a pinch of logic.

by Russ Carpenter

There is no need to forgo good food on a fishing or hunting trip, even when such a trip takes you far from the luxuries of a permanent camp or commercial lakeside lodge. The success of wilderness cooking depends on what is carried in the grub box, what is added from Nature's bounty, what is done before and during cooking, and what kind of heat is used.

For good taste and variety, I pack canned vegetables, dry soup mixes, bouillon cubes (or powder), bacon, shortening, and plenty of condiments: salt, pepper, poultry seasoning, garlic salt. I also carry flour—some of it preseasoned with salt and pepper—baking powder, and baking soda. Onions are another must, and fresh carrots, potatoes, and celery are great in many dishes. With these ingredients and with what the rod or gun can provide, fine camp meals are in the offing.

In the summer, for example, whether I'm on a short hike or a long fishing trip I carry a little take-down fly rod that provides food as well as sport. Nothing is tastier than small trout, fresh from a mountain stream, sautéed in butter or bacon drippings. When fish are too small for filleting, too delicate for conventional frying, I prepare them for sautéing by simply cleaning the cavity, leaving the head, fins, and tail attached. Then I wipe each one dry and roll it in preseasoned flour. The fire should be medium, not extremely hot, and it is better to be a trifle skimpy than overgenerous with the bacon fat or butter. To satisfy hungry hikers, you need at least three small trout per serving, and they will brown nicely in ten to twelve minutes.

To feed a party in the bush or on the lee shore of some remote island, I carry two frying pans, a four-quart and a six-quart kettle, and, if the weight can be managed, a Dutch oven. If the place is rocky, I build a simple rock fireplace; otherwise I build the fire in a hole in the ground. Rocks must be dry, or they may crack or even explode. A wire grill makes the stove top. However, if the packing-in of extra equipment is no problem, I follow the lead of most guides and use a portable camp stove.

Heat must be fairly uniform for good cooking results. Modern camp stoves are adjustable, but a campfire requires close attention. For some purposes, a very hot fire is needed, so the flames must be moderately high, but for other jobs hot coals are required. If several pots and pans are to be placed on the grill or hung over the coals at once, the fire must be wide and long enough to accommodate all of them. It is odd how many otherwise skillful woodsmen build a puny fire under the rear area of a grill and then try to spread the coals

PHOTOGRAPH BY J. BARRY O'ROURKE

forward, usually while sucking on a burned finger, to get the vegetables done by the time the meat is ready.

For campfire cooking on a fishing trip, I particularly recommend fillet of walleye, northern pike, smallmouth bass, or lake trout, fried the old-fashioned way in deep, hot fat. I like to eat these fish with only bread and butter, washed down with hot tea if the weather is chilly, or with good Canadian ale if it's warm. For a larger meal, I pan-fry a few potatoes, heat some vegetables, and present a bush-country version of fish and chips.

To prepare fillets neatly and quickly, lay the fish on its side on a board or log and with a knife (preferably not too sharp since it must be worked under the skin without cutting through) cut to the backbone just behind the head. Then turn the blade toward the tail and with a sawing motion cut along the backbone almost to the tail. Turn the cut piece back over the tail and saw back toward the first cut, sliding the knife between the flesh and the skin. This gives you the fillet from one side. Turn the fish over and repeat the operation on the other side. The backbone, viscera, head, and skin are still attached to each other and ready to feed to the ravens.

In the grub box on my fishing trips I carry a can with enough lard or bacon grease to give me an inch or more of hot oil for frying. I put the fillets into a bag of flour preseasoned with salt and pepper, and shake it to give the fish a good coating. The fire must be hot because the secret of deep-frying is hot oil. To test the oil, drop in a small piece of bread, which should start to brown in about a minute. If it doesn't, more heat is needed. You can make the same test with a very small chunk of fish; it should bubble and sizzle, and quickly start browning. When the oil is hot enough, put in the fillets. When they are golden-brown, immediately remove and drain them.

Some outdoor cooks always sprinkle a little mild paprika on the fillets before frying them, which turns the fish a slightly richer brown. However, I think the use of such spices should depend on your taste preferences rather than on the resultant color.

While the oil is heating, there is plenty of time to open a can of vegetables and set it close to the fire to heat. (If you use fresh vegetables, put them on to boil before filleting the fish, because they take longer to cook.) This is also the time to peel and thinly slice a few potatoes, and fry them in hot oil in a second pan, or in the fish pan if you're cooking for a small party and there's room enough. Both the fish and the chips should be liberally salted after they are cooked.

To break the monotony of fried food, poached fish—especially salmon, landlocked salmon, or large trout—are delightful. Poaching requires forethought, because you must have a piece of cheesecloth in which to wrap the fish and a large kettle. Trout and salmon are usually poached whole, though the head and tail can be removed if the kettle is small.

After wrapping the cleaned fish in cheesecloth, prepare enough poaching liquid so that it will cover the fish. To each quart of water add a tablespoon of salt, two sliced or diced carrots, a chopped onion, a chopped stalk of celery, pepper to taste, a bay leaf, a cup of white wine, and a slice of lemon. Boil the liquid for a few minutes to blend the ingredients, then lower the fish into it, bring it to a boil again, and lower the temperature (or raise the kettle higher above the fire), so that it will gently simmer until done. A three-pound landlocked salmon takes about twenty-five minutes to cook. Poached fish is best when it is served with melted butter.

Fish chowder is another delicacy that lends itself to camp preparation, but care must be taken to prevent it from turning into a mushy mixture of fish crumbs in milk. Though white perch has the perfect texture, consistency, and taste for chowder, this dish is all the better if the perch is used in combination with other firm-fleshed species. Salmon and bass are perhaps the best candidates.

In water seasoned with salt and pepper, gently boil the fish until it will flake. Remove the small, thin pieces first and keep taking out successively larger pieces as soon as they are cooked. Flake the fish and set it aside, saving the liquid. Dice four slices of bacon or salt pork and brown them in a kettle. After removing the bacon, sauté a chopped onion and a chopped red tomato in the grease. (Some outdoorsmen object to carrying easily crushed items such as tomatoes, but they can be worth a bit of packing ingenuity.) Dice four or five potatoes, add them to the pot with the browned bacon or pork, and pour in enough of the poaching liquid to cover. After cooking this for about ten minutes, thicken it with a little flour blended in butter and simmer for another three minutes. Now add enough milk for the desired serving consistency and finally—last of all—add the flaked fish and simmer the chowder for three more minutes.

If you run out of certain vegetables or wish to vary the flavor of a particular recipe, you can often improvise in the wilderness, especially during the summer months when wild plants are ripening. Wild onions have a slightly different taste than any of the domestic varieties and are equally delicious either raw as garnishes and in salads or cooked in poached dishes and chowders.

Breakfast can test the camp cook's ingenuity and resources. Eggs may become tiresome, and will present packing problems. Fewer eggs will be needed if they are used as ingredients, rather than as the main course.

Breakfasts can be varied with delicious whole-wheat sourdough flapjacks (as well as breads or biscuits). Some outdoor chefs continually add to the sourdough "starter" and keep it alive interminably, claiming that it gets better as it ages.

To make sourdough starter, mix a pack of dry yeast, a cup of whole-wheat flour, and a cup of warm water in a crock or glass jar—*not* in anything made of metal. Let the mixture stand for one day in a warm spot, covered lightly with a cloth; and that night add another two cups of whole-wheat flour and two more cups of warm water, again mixing the ingredients. Let the mixture stand overnight.

For a flapjack breakfast, put two cups of the starter into a bowl, add two eggs, a tablespoon of salt, a tablespoon of sugar, and a scant teaspoon of baking soda. Some cooks prefer to enhance the flavor by adding two tablespoons of bacon drippings. Spoon this onto a hot griddle so that each flapjack spreads out to five or six inches across, brown nicely on both sides, and serve with pats of butter and warm maple syrup. Be sure to save some of the starter for future use.

When the fishing and hunting seasons overlap, a man's thoughts stray from the aroma of browned trout to that of well-cooked upland birds. They are among the things that make up the good life, and they are surprisingly easy to prepare. A few years ago I camped with Larry Koller and wildlife photographer Gordon Eastman high in the Wyoming mountains, next to an emerald-green pond appropriately named Jewel Lake. Along the trail Larry potted a couple of sage hens which weren't the youngest, tenderest birds imaginable—but he had a knack with whatever was at hand.

He cut them into serving pieces and simmered them for several hours in a kettle of water with a cut-up onion and some salt and pepper. Then he removed them and added a packet of dry cream-of-onion soup mix, plus a little flour-and-water mixture to thicken the stock. When it had cooked down to the consistency of gravy, he returned the birds to the kettle and set it near the edge of the campfire to keep it warm until we were ready to eat. Since that day I've used the same recipe, sometimes with variations, both at home and on the trail. Almost any kind of bird, or several species cooked together, will work beautifully. Chopped celery can be added to the simmering stock, cream-of-leek soup mix is excellent in place of cream-of-onion, and a bit of sherry is a welcome addition to the cooked-down gravy.

The ruffed grouse, king of game birds not only in the coverts but on the table, provides little to eat other than its thick white breast, but this is enough to concentrate on. I open up the skin to expose the meat and, with a sharp knife, cut down along the breastbone and out to the side. This filleting operation gives me a piece of delicate white meat from each side. I split them partly through and open them, just as a butcher opens a veal cutlet. I slap each partridge cutlet flat with the knife blade, then rub in flour seasoned with salt and pepper. Over a slow fire, the cutlets are fried in butter or margarine until they are golden-brown.

When the big-game seasons open, I rely on venison recipes that work as nicely with sheep, goat, elk, moose, and some other species. It is advisable to let a carcass hang, cooling, for at least a day after the kill. Because cooking time in a deer camp may be stolen from hunting time, I like dinners that can be prepared at night for the following day. If there's an oven in camp, I make hunter's pie. If there's no oven, I substitute dumplings for the crust, and the same basic stew is then a Mulligan. At least half a pound of meat is needed per serving, and I'll give directions to feed six hungry hunters.

Cut up three pounds of trimmed venison into about one-inch chunks. Using three tablespoons of bacon grease, brown the meat in a big skillet or Dutch oven. Add four or five medium onions cut into quarters, a pint of tomatoes, a can of beer, a cup of double-strength beef bouillon, and two bay leaves. Simmer until the venison begins to get tender. Unless you're using a Dutch oven, you then transfer the food to a kettle. Add five peeled and quartered potatoes, four or five sliced carrots, and a can of peas. Simmer on a low fire while you make dough, which can be the same for dumplings or crust.

Mix two cups of flour, three teaspoons of sugar, three teaspoons of baking powder, a little over half a teaspoon of salt, a cup of milk, an egg, and four tablespoons of oil or melted shortening. If it isn't smooth, add a bit more milk.

For a hunter's pie, spoon this onto the simmering stew and bake it, *uncovered*, in a hot oven (about 425 degrees) for about twenty-five minutes. For a Mulligan with dumplings, simmer the stew an extra ten minutes, then add the dough a spoon at a time, dipping the spoon into the stew before adding each glob so the dough will slide off easily. Cover it, and simmer for about twenty-five minutes. You can add to this from day to day, making new crusts or dumplings. It seems to improve with each successive warming up.

This recipe for big-game stew or pie can also be applied to small game. Rabbit or squirrel is excellent this way. The meat should be cut up and browned, just like venison, before stewing. If small furred game is sufficiently young and tender, it can also be fixed in the same way as game birds. A little improvisation—varying ingredients to suit a desire for a particular seasoning or vegetable, substituting one kind of meat for another—will enrich the fare on any fishing or hunting expedition.

busy. It is when you step inside the air terminal that you know you are in the North. Nearly everyone in the waiting room is a sportsman. The baggage area is crowded with gun cases and fishing rods, boxes of caribou quarters and freshly caught salmon. Antlers are piled high and tagged for flight back to Montreal; most of the racks measure more than three feet high. The sportsmen coming in meet the sportsmen going out. Racks are examined and advice to the newcomers flows in torrents: fly patterns are recommended, water levels on various rivers are compared, and hunting tips are offered. "Don't shoot the first big rack you see," they tell you. "They all look big at first, but the biggest racks are often spotted after you've shot a smaller trophy."

We flew by float plane from Schefferville to Fritz Gregor's DePas River camp, eighty-eight miles to the northeast. Fritz operates the Montagnais Hunting and Fishing Club which has eight comfortable camps in the Ungava. The little bush planes that ferry sportsmen to the Ungava camps are kept busiest in July and September, for in July the salmon fishing is almost matched by the trout fishing, and in September, when the caribou season is open, the summer salmon run is still in progress and a later run has also begun.

Our flight took us over rugged terrain. Barren rock mountains hunched up amid thousands of long lakes. In the valleys, spruces grow in black profusion, but from the mountain shoulders to the summits growth is limited to ankle height. The bare mountaintops are covered with the light gray-green caribou moss and lichens, which are the primary foods of the big deer of the North.

From the air you see the game trails. An endless tracery of black lines carves the tundra into a million pieces like a puzzle that has been loosely put together. These trails scar the hillsides for years after they are created. The huge cloven hoofs of the caribou, as large across as those of a moose, cut through the lichens and mosses to the rock below. The extremely slow growth rate of these plants in northern latitudes requires ten to twelve years before the tracks are obliterated. This is true also of the plants upon which caribou have browsed. If a large herd feeds over an area, it can trample and eat enough of the lichens and mosses to limit that area's grazing potential for years to come. Thus caribou must keep on the move almost constantly.

Our camp was a comfortable two-room wooden building—a bunk room and a large kitchen with dining area presided over by a camp cook. Overlooking a wide sweep of the DePas River below barren hills, the camp is an outpost of civilization in an awesome, wild landscape. On the beach in front of the camp were tracks of caribou, made the day before. Nearby in the wet sand was the track of a hunting wolf.

On our first morning, photographer Hanson Carroll and I boarded a 22-foot freight canoe with our guide, Leo Poitras, and were taken three miles upstream. The river, two hundred yards wide in most places, was low and the sun was bright. Such conditions, pleasant though they were, did not indicate good salmon fishing. Usually the weather is cold and the skies are gray. Water levels fluctuate and conditions change day by day. This was, however, an ideal day to hunt, and it was possible that I might see a trophy before midday.

Leo poled, paddled, and motored us up long stretches of rapids where the tundra-covered hills swoop down to the spruce-heavy river valley. We stopped at a bend in the river where the hills above us looked like high New England sheep pastures. Skirting through a fringe of spruces, we climbed through dwarf willow and berry bushes for a few hundred yards and emerged on the barren but mossy uplands. As we followed a deeply cut caribou trail to the summit, we scanned the rocky outcroppings for movement. At the top we crouched in the sweet, spicy-smelling caribou moss and began searching the hillsides which stretched away to the horizon.

"We will see many caribou from here," Leo told us. We had climbed only fifteen minutes from the river bank.

In a moment the first caribou appeared. At one instant there had been only a rocky summit on the hill ahead of us, but at the next a caribou was framed against the sky. It was a cow, chocolate-coated, with short jutting antlers poking above her head like pieces of jagged driftwood; caribou cows are the only female members of the deer family that grow antlers. Behind her came a young bull, and I saw at once why we had been warned against shooting the first bull we spotted. The guide shook his head negatively, although the animal had a rack easily three feet high, with a broad shovel sweeping out vertically from his forehead. To one accustomed to looking at whitetail deer, he seemed gigantic.

"Small one," Leo muttered disdainfully. "Wait, we'll see the rest of the herd now." Then, after a long pause, he said, "Look, here comes a good one for sure."

Above the summit of the hill, the top of a rack was emerging. The antlers looked at first like a wind-twisted willow bush with its leaves turned up and over by the wind. But this was no willow bush. The rack rose higher and higher over the summit, revealing a wide bow. The top tines were long, jutting up with a forward curl; halfway down the main beam, another branch appeared. Then the big bull's head popped over the top, revealing a heavy brow shovel and the whitened face of an old campaigner.

This was a herd bull. He mounted the summit, silhouetting himself against the sky, and raised his muzzle so that the long antlers lay back along his flanks as he tested the wind. His coat was whitened by age and the sun, and his powerful neck bulged with a hump of muscle.

We were hardly more than a hundred yards from the old bull, in plain sight but downwind of him. He looked directly at us and began to circle to get our scent. This is a common maneuver in regions where caribou have not developed the intense fear of man that marks other members of the deer family. The caribou's enemy is the wolf, and even the wolf is dangerous only to very young animals or old, weak ones. The bull showed only curiosity and caution, not fear. He bounded along the slope parallel to us with the graceful high-kneed trot of his clan, muzzle outstretched, antlers back along his sides. His fluid rhythm took him over the broken, rocky ground as if he were floating in slow motion across a movie screen.

He stopped perhaps a hundred and fifty yards away, still unable to get our scent. Throughout his display, I had held my rifle on him, studying him through the scope, but I had no desire to shoot a caribou the first morning, regardless of how fine a bull he was.

"His antlers are good but not a real trophy," Leo said. "He has only the single shovel. And his meat will be very strong."

Caribou venison is excellent—tender, well-covered with fat, and mild-tasting. It can substitute for beef in any recipe. But the old bulls have a strong flavor which some people would call gamy. I had decided to hunt for a good bull with nice antlers, but I also wanted fine venison to take home. A fat four- or five-year-old bull with an impressive head was what I wanted.

The old bull dashed over the top of a hill and disappeared, but then his curiosity drove him back and we spotted him sneak-

Water sprays from coat of Ungava caribou as animal, alarmed by photographer, bounds from river's edge toward protective brush.

ing in on us from another angle. Several times he reared on his hind legs and whirled and dashed away, only to come trotting back in his high-kneed prance.

"He is almost in the rut," Leo said. "He begins to act crazy for the females."

Like all the caribou we saw in Ungava during early September, he was still in velvet. But already he was feeling the urge which, by the end of the month, would cause him to gather a harem and to fight viciously with any rival bulls. By September, caribou antlers have reached full growth, and the thin hairy membrane which covers them is ready to slough off in long strips when the animal engages in mock battles with the twisted branches of dwarf willows. October is the rutting month, and by then the shooting season has passed. For about six weeks, the bulls engage in a continual orgy of battling other bulls and breeding the dozen or so cows in their harems. During the breeding season, the males have little time or inclination to eat. By the end of the month, they are gouged and torn, weakened and wasted.

In September, however, just before the rut begins, the animals are prime; sleek and fat after a summer of easy living and abundant feed. The hindquarters are covered with layers of fat up to three inches thick, the ribs filled out and round as the barrel of a horse. The caribou of this region range from two hundred to four hundred pounds, and the best hunting arms are therefore rifles of .270 caliber or larger, using bullets of at least 150 grains. Shotguns are not permitted in caribou camps.

We found bands of the animals each day on the DePas River. They were always cautious, but seemed to feel safe enough so long as they could keep a couple of hundred yards away from us. No day went by without our spotting good bulls. A hunter can never know what problems he may encounter, but with a scope-sighted rifle in the open tundra, a kill is often fairly easy—once you have found the trophy you want.

Mine appeared late one afternoon while I was fishing a smooth piece of water a mile below our camp. I saw the bull come down to the water half a mile upstream, and a quick check through 8x30 binoculars showed him to be fat. He had a tall, symmetrical rack and his coat was brownish-gray. Deciding to try for him, I ran to the canoe as the bull stepped into the water and began swimming across. While we were speeding upstream, I exchanged my fly rod for a sporterized Springfield .30/06 and pressed four 180-grain cartridges into the magazine. When the bull neared shore, Leo turned the canoe and ran it aground. The caribou was galloping up the shoreline seventy-five yards away. I chambered a shell and put the cross hairs on the back of his upraised neck. The boom of the shot combined with a walloping thud as the 375-pound bull fell dead at the edge of the willows.

Dressing the bull and dragging him back to the water's edge was done with such ease that we didn't realize how difficult this chore can be under other circumstances. We learned about that the next day when Hanson Carroll collected a similar bull on the backside of a ridge two steep miles from the river.

We had hunted along the ridge where the old herd bull had been spotted on our first morning. From the summit of the barren rock mountain, the tundra stretched away into a valley where the early-morning light sparkled on a small lake rimmed with spruces. White frost glistened on the dwarf willows, and shrouds of mist rose from the eastern sides of the sun-washed hills. In the distance stood regiments of black mountains. We swept the valley with binoculars and finally spotted a caribou calf grazing on the slope of the next mountain.

"That calf will be near to a herd," Leo said. "We'll go over there and look in the next valley."

We walked down the long slope, slipping on the spongy, sweet-smelling tundra, wading through a swamp where the twisted willows tangled our feet and caught at our clothes. Emerging from the bush, we found the calf grazing near a hilltop a quarter-mile ahead. Quickly we climbed above the brushy draws and came into the rolling tundra. We followed a low gully across the face of the hill, keeping out of sight of the calf.

When we were barely a hundred yards from her, we glassed the valley again, but still saw no other caribou. The calf, about the size of a whitetail doe, now saw us but her curiosity overcame her caution and she bounded a few yards toward us. She then cut downhill, circled, disappeared into the gully, reappeared several hundred yards away, and bounded away over the ridge.

"She'll spook the herd for sure," Leo commented. "They'll watch for us now."

We reached the summit in time to see eight or nine caribou trot into the bush in the next valley. Ten minutes later we spotted them again, swinging along in a brushy draw. Then they broke out onto the tundra on the slope of a mountain about half a mile from us. Several had tall racks but they were too far away for us to assess them accurately. Once more we headed down a long slope, clawed our way through the boggy, brush-choked lowlands, and climbed into the open where we could glass the herd. There were three bulls, and all of them had the combination of handsome rack and well-fattened young body we sought. The calf had alerted the herd, but they had not seen or scented us yet. After a minute's rest, Hanson slung the Springfield over his shoulder and we circled toward a ridge that rose above the animals. The stalk continued like that for over an hour as we worked back into the hills more than two miles from the river.

Finally Hans bellied ahead of us toward a summit, raised his head over a rock, and looked into the face of a caribou cow only thirty yards away. She plunged downhill, sending the rest of the herd into a panic, and they raced across a hillside. At nearly two hundred yards, the fat double-shoveled bull that Hans had chosen separated himself from the herd and offered a clean though difficult shot as he trotted up the slope alone. Sitting, Hans braced the rifle across his knees, put the cross hairs on the front of the bull's chest, and fired. The bull toppled, crashing into the low brush.

It was a fine, heavy bull of four or five years, with handsome antlers and twin vertical brow shovels. Leo dressed the animal, skinned out the hindquarters, and cut them away at the loin. Now the job was to get our prize back to the canoe. Leo carried the 120-pound hind section on his shoulders while Hans and I dragged the rest of the animal. Going downhill, we pulled on the antlers and the carcass skated along behind. But when we got to the swampy, flat bottoms and into the tangling bush, perspiration began to pour. The antlers caught in brush and we stumbled frequently. The uphill drags were tougher still, even after we attached a leather tumpline to the antlers. The sun was high now and the early-morning frost had melted away. Our smashing through the bush seemed to awaken hordes of black flies and mosquitoes, and the heat of our bodies drew them to us. It was afternoon when we got the carcass to the river bank and sprawled on the rocks.

"Now," said Leo, grinning, "you see what caribou hunting is like. One day you shoot the bull at the river's edge. Another day you kill him but you almost kill yourself, too."

Because of the caribou's unpredictable grazing pattern, the herd you see one morning may be miles away the next morning. On the other hand, a hillside that's rich in deep caribou moss may hold a herd for several days. To scout for a record head, the hunter will usually have to spend much time combing the slopes and slogging through the swamps between the upland stretches. Caribou are daylight feeders, grazing from dawn until late morning and again from about four in the afternoon until dark. More caribou are seen at the river's edge late in the afternoon than at any other time. It is also well to remember that a hillside which shows very fresh tracks and droppings is likely to be a grazing spot again the following morning.

When frightened, a caribou can move with amazing speed. They have been clocked at thirty miles an hour over rough terrain. But once a bull has put a couple of ridges between himself and a hunter, he resumes grazing. Thus, a trophy caribou that has been spooked can generally be followed up half an hour later, but of course the stalk becomes much more difficult when the quarry is nervous. We had learned that lesson well by the time Hans got his shot.

After returning to camp with our meat, we sat down to a dinner of fried caribou liver and onions. We were jubilant. Our hunt had been successful, and the next day we would be on the salmon waters.

I don't know why I put off for so long my personal introduction to the stately Atlantic salmon. I had taken my share of hefty brown trout on tiny flies in New England. I'd landed big Maine squaretails on June evenings when the brown drakes pop through the surface film of mountain lakes and a quietly presented Wulff-tied dry is potent. I knew the stealth that brings success on mountain streams where brook trout feed at dawn. My schooling had been arduous on landlocked salmon streams and lakes. I'd even ventured north and taken arctic char and monster speckled trout on bright flies under the tutelage of Eskimos. In short, I considered myself a fisherman of fair experience. Yet I'd never met the grandest fish of all.

My introduction to *Salmo salar* came on the DePas River, a few hundred yards from where I'd shot my caribou. Nothing can surpass the thrill I felt the first time I saw a hook-jawed old cock salmon, resplendent in spawning colors, rise to my fly and then sink slowly back upon his lie. It wasn't just his size or the color of him that made my breath come short; it was the slow, deliberate way in which he came for the fly—pushing a bow wave across the slow glide of the current, thrusting up to within a foot of my bright bucktail, his beaked lower jaw slanting down in a white line—and the way he settled back toward the bottom with a dignified air of refusal. There was no splash, no frenzied rush, only calculated curiosity.

"Hey, he's a good one for sure," Leo shouted from the bank. To Leo, everything positive is "for sure."

"What now?" I asked, afraid of making a mistake and spoiling this august ceremony we were conducting to tempt a salmon to take hold.

Leo shrugged. "Maybe you try a smaller fly."

"Bright or dark?" I was nervous. Everything I had learned about taking fish seemed to have escaped me. Any pattern Leo suggested I would use. He had caught salmon by the thousands, and this was the first I'd ever seen. Leo would know what to do.

"Probably one either of dark color or bright maybe will work," Leo ventured. He wasn't saying "for sure" anymore.

Books had taught me that when a salmon rises but does not take, the angler should change flies and try again. For the moment, however, this booklearning was ignored since I had no idea what fly to change to. Excitedly I rolled out a cast, lifted it high in back of me, and sent the same bucktail sailing over the water. I let it sink for a few seconds in the current and then began a slow retrieve that would swim the Tri-Color past the same spot.

The sweep of my line showed that the fly was nearing the spot where the salmon had risen. He came again. A black bulge of water pushed up behind the fly and I saw the salmon coming. I saw him open his big white mouth—open it wide enough to take a muskrat—and I struck! Everything in me reacted and I yanked back on the rod and pulled the bucktail skittering across the surface two feet ahead of the sedate fish.

"You scare him for sure that way," Leo observed.

I never saw that salmon again. During the course of the afternoon I learned three basic ways to scare salmon without hurting them. I had already put one fish down by yanking the fly away from a rise. The next one departed with a fly in his jaw when I struck to set the hook. You don't strike salmon. You tighten up when they hit and let them hook themselves as they turn away.

"You give him too much the horse," Leo remarked.

The third fish never got a look at the fly. I sent him flashing off in terror by wading directly into his lie before covering the water ahead of me with careful casts.

"First you fish in the water," said Leo. "Later you walk in it."

Late that afternoon, when the shadows of the jagged spruces lengthened on the water and the breeze came down from the hills

Author tails fat, fresh-run salmon in DePas River, less than two miles downstream from camp.

with a feeling of snow, I got another chance. The water was a long, smooth glide a hundred yards below a shallow rapids. About four feet of water slid over a dark bottom covered with rocks the size of a man's fist and littered with heavy boulders. The current moved at a half-walk speed. The surface was almost glassy, with just a little turbulence around boulders.

I began with short casts and gradually lengthened them. Three dozen times I swam the fly past the tail of a boulder that caught my eye across the current and just a bit below me. I had learned one thing for all of my mistakes that afternoon. A salmon isn't like a trout. Sometimes a salmon will watch a fly go past countless times and refuse it and then, for no apparent reason, rise and take, long after you have convinced yourself that casting is useless and the only reason to continue is that your guide expects you to.

That was how it was. I'd shown my fly to every inch of water within casting range dozens of times over. Then, as the fly drifted past the back of the boulder for perhaps the fortieth time, there was a slight disturbance and the curve of my line straightened and pulled up out of the water with little droplets springing from it.

Pinching the line against the cork grip with my forefinger, I raised the rod tip steadily and felt the big fish embed the hook deeply into his jaw as he turned against the tightening pull. For a moment he seemed confused by the restraint of the hook. I felt him throbbing and moving slowly away across the current. I gave a small amount of line and kept moderate pressure on the fish. Then he made up his mind to rid himself of the irritating hook, and took off. He smashed through the surface and leaped, shining silver, heaving spray as he wrenched his heavy body into the air and fell back with a crash upon the surface. Five times he jumped, arcing three feet into the air, carrying his fight out toward the middle of the wide river.

Mentally I prepared myself for the long downstream run guaranteed in the angling books. My reel was loaded with a hundred and fifty yards of backing for this eventuality. Later I would learn that there are no certainties in salmon fishing. No two fish behave alike. This one never made the long run. He counted on high jumps and bulldozer dives to the bottom to free himself. Gradually I worked him closer to the rock on which I stood. When he saw me, the fish made a short dash upstream and thrashed on top. But I had an advantage, for in the faster water upstream the salmon had to fight the current as well as the rod. Slowly he exhausted himself, and finally his rolls on the surface were tired ones and the danger was only that he would roll himself in the leader and twist the hook free. In ten minutes I drew the spent fish into the wide mouth of Leo's waiting net.

Such was my first Atlantic salmon. Thirty inches long, he weighed an ounce or two below nine pounds. Not big as salmon go, he was nonetheless my first. On his cheeks a heavy blush of red broke through in crimson freckles. His sides were dark with vivid red spots. His tail, wide as a shovel, had a pink flare; his hooked lower jaw was almost sinister.

"He is bright now," Leo said, "and he is strong but not fat. He first comes to the mouth of the river in July. Through the summer he moves upstream each time the rains come and the water rises. He does not eat but lives on his fat—like a hibernating bear in winter. His colors keep changing and getting brighter.

"The July fish have been in the river all summer and now commence the spawning," Leo explained. "Through September and early October the spawning continues. Many

of the fish are already here, but with the next rains should come more salmon fresh from the ocean."

The DePas River is a tributary of northern Quebec's famous George River. It runs from a point northeast of Schefferville for nearly a hundred and fifty miles north to Indian House Lake and joins the George just below the lake. The DePas is a new salmon river. When we were there in September, it had been fished by only two parties before us. Its full potential is still to be explored. All that is known is that it gets a heavy run of salmon in July and another heavy run in September. The fish rarely weigh less than eight pounds, and anglers have now taken them in excess of fifteen pounds. The average is between nine and eleven pounds, and there are plenty of these salmon.

Where Fritz Gregor's camp is located, the river is wide—two hundred yards on the average. Within five miles upstream and down are stretches of water that would delight any salmon fisherman. Near the camp are three sets of rapids separated by slow, flat places half a mile long. Below the rapids are pools studded with boulders where the current eases and a salmon can rest before making its next onslaught against the rushing current. It is in such places that salmon are most often caught.

One can stand on the dock and see salmon jump, but Leo Poitras does not fish his parties there. "The fish are only moving through that stretch," he says. "They will not take the fly. Me, I'll take you where they bite."

Why salmon jump is a mystery. Some say it is to rid themselves of the irritating sea lice that cling to their tail sections when they first arrive from the sea. Others claim that male salmon fight, and that occasionally one of them jumps while fleeing from another one. Another strange phenomenon is that there are places, as Leo points out, where salmon are seen regularly but never caught. To catch them, you must find their lies, resting spots where they hold before making an exhausting run up the next rapids, or a place where the bottom is covered with fist-sized stones below a slow current—a spawning area.

As a trout fisherman, I would have passed the best lies by and fished the faster water or floated a dry fly over the deeper pools, just those places where Leo said salmon would not hit. At one productive spot, a single rock jutted from the shore inside the curve of the river where it flattened out below a rapids and swooped into a long, deep curve. The water for a hundred yards was three or four feet deep, with a soft current and no particular place where a trout fisherman would say, "There, by that rock, the water forms a channel where the fish will feed on morsels carried by the flow."

The hardest thing to remember on salmon waters is that the fish are there to breed and not to feed. Although salmon can often be observed taking natural flies and nymphs, the food is rarely swallowed. The fish evidently takes the insect because of a response that has lingered since the salmon was a small parr. Now back in the river of its heritage, it responds to the old urge and rises to an insect, sucks it in—then spits it out. The stomachs of salmon in fresh water are usually empty. I had no luck at any spot that looked like a feeding station, and Leo taught me to search for places where the salmon could lie on their pectoral fins along the bottom.

When the sun was bright on the water, we took a couple of fish, but real success came whenever the weather turned. When the sky was heavy with looming snow clouds, and white flakes pelted us and a stiff wind riffled the surface, we had the best fishing. The day before we left, the river rose a foot and a half following a heavy rain. Despite mixed rain and sleet, we went out on the broad river on our last day and in two hours took two bright salmon—8½ and 10¼ pounds—harbingers of the late run which was just beginning on that high water.

For the most part, we took fish on #4 long-shanked Tri-Color bucktails. Although these orange, green, and white creations are not typical salmon flies, the brilliant colors seemed to attract fish consistently. However, Leo's favorite fly is a red and white bucktail, or a red and yellow Mickey Finn. Number 4 bucktails are big beside the average salmon fly, but on the DePas a big fly works best. We tried salmon patterns such as the Rusty Rat, Black Dose, Durham Ranger, Thunder and Lightning, Jock Scott —all good producers on the nearby George River—without success. The big bright bucktails were apparently just right for local conditions.

For general fishing, the best month on the DePas is probably July. Then the first salmon run is new in the river, and the big speckled trout and lake trout feed voraciously in the rapids. Late in August the speckled trout move up into smaller brooks to spawn and the lakers head for deep holes along the river's course. In September, the DePas is strictly a salmon river, loaded with fish which have grown colorful and just begun to spawn. And as the water rises each night, new salmon move up the river.

At this time of year, the weather is uncertain, and your bush pilot may inform you that you will have to delay as much as a day in Schefferville. You must nevertheless pay for the time you have booked at the camp, but if bad weather delays the flight *out* of camp, the extra time on the river is free. Like most aspects of fishing, it's a gamble.

The camp operators do not believe in making guests rough it in the wilderness. There is even plenty of fresh domestic meat on the menu, but few sportsmen will choose beef when the meat rack is hung with caribou and the moss pit holds newly caught salmon. Our camp cook delighted in serving caribou and salmon dinners. There's nothing like fresh salmon steaks broiled over a spruce-knot fire at the river's edge in the middle of the day when you are questing after adventure in a northern wild land. And adventure is the proper word. Even though a man may schedule his hunting in the early morning and his fishing in the afternoon, he must be prepared for the unexpected at all times. It is wise to keep both fishing tackle and a rifle handy, for in this genuine wilderness there is no way to tell when the salmon may become ravenous or a trophy caribou may wander to the water's edge. ◉

CONTINUED FROM PAGE 27

cooperative hunting club in New Jersey. But by profession and inclination I am a wildlife photographer. Studying and photographing wildlife at close range is the consuming interest of my life. And it seems to me that any really serious student of wild animals simply must go to East Africa.

Like many hunters, I have always felt that the actual kill—the instant of the shot—is far from the most important aspect of the hunt. Being at one with the natural environment, stalking the animals and studying their ways, these are the elements that matter most. Where big and unusual game abounds, one can sometimes have just as much excitement without a gun. I have approached an irascible bull elephant, attracted the stare of a wallowing Cape buffalo, taken pictures within scant yards of wild lions as they stalked and fed. My best lion photos were taken at a distance of twelve feet. Few hunters ever come that close to a splendid black-maned lion, or a prime, tawny lioness. And since my trophies are pictures there is no limit on their number, legal or otherwise.

The wealth and diversity of East African wildlife is incredible—lions, leopards, cheetahs, wild hunting dogs, hyenas, jackals, elephants, rhinos, hippos, gazelles, baboons, monkeys, brilliantly colored birds of countless species. For the photographic trophy hunter, Africa's huge and truly wild national parks are ideal stalking grounds. Kenya's Tsavo National Park, which dwarfs even America's Yellowstone, is the largest in the world. Tsavo has over thirty thousand elephants. My party, traveling fifty-five hundred miles through Kenya, Tanzania, and Uganda on a sixty-day safari, visited nine other parks as well: Amboseli, Mara Masai, Ngorongoro Crater, Serengeti Plains, Lake Manyara, Queen Elizabeth, Murchison Falls, Lake Nukuru, and Nairobi. Along the way I took over ninety-five hundred pictures.

My companions were a friend of mine named Richard Nilsen, a professional guide named Finn Allan, and Mwetu Juma, an African safari hand who performed most of the chores and served as camp cook. Through the Clara Laughlin Travel Agency in New York, I had contacted Don Turner, a tour operator in Nairobi. Don is a well-known ornithologist who conducts birding tours that are generally booked solid. His usual type of expedition was not what I had in mind, but I knew that he would be willing to act as outfitter. He provided our guide and camp hand, and he also supplied our Land Rover, food, petrol, and camping equipment. It will surprise many an old African hunter to learn that the cost of the sixty-day safari for Rich and me came to $5,000, plus airfare. This was because both of us, having camped enough in the American wilderness to be used to a rugged outdoor life, had agreed to dispense with such safari luxuries as a daily change of bed linen, daily laundering service, and portable bathtubs.

Then, too, we did not have to buy the hunting licenses or pay the additional fees required of hunters who shoot antelopes, gazelles, or one of the big-five game animals—lion, leopard, Cape buffalo, elephant, and rhino. Depending on the country and the species, these fees run from $100 to $500. By forgoing the conventional kind of trophies, I also saved the high taxidermy and shipping expenses, and was able to take along an immense amount of photographic equipment and film. Furthermore, I was able to do my hunting in game-rich park areas that are closed to conventional hunters.

When photographing wildlife in East African parks, one is usually required by law to stay in a vehicle. This is not to say that I remained in the Land Rover during the entire safari, or that I did not encounter all sorts of game while on foot around our campsites. But park visitors are unarmed and it could be extremely dangerous to walk through some areas. Actually, the vehicle permitted us to get closer to the game than we could have stalked on foot. Most wild animals do not feel threatened by a vehicle and therefore make no great effort to hide or run when a car comes close. Occasionally, however, they do consider a vehicle to be an intrusion, which means there is always the possibility of attack.

I'll never forget our first encounter with a rhino. It was in an area of Tsavo National Park—covering about four thousand square miles—which is restricted to one party per day. I was exhilarated by the realization that my companions and I were the only human beings in these vast wilds. Driving along the dusty road—a trail, really—we encountered two bull rhinos having a difference of opinion, probably over territorial rights. Amid a great deal of puffing and snorting, they pretended to charge each other, but always stopped short of collision. After about ten minutes of this posturing and bluffing, the larger rhino finally drove the smaller one away into the brush. During this display we had kept our motor running and the big remaining rhino now heard it and noticed us, apparently for the first time. Ordinarily—in spite of hair-raising stories—the rhinoceros is not a truculent beast, but his great curiosity can get him into trouble. Having poor eyesight, but an acute sense of smell and hearing, a rhino will sense the presence of a strange object or animal and will dash up to get a better look, stomping over anything in the way.

After routing his opponent, this one was in a triumphantly belligerent mood. For a moment he stood in the road with his head extended, nostrils and prehensile lip working to get our scent. With tail held high, he trotted toward us, stopped, and turned sideways to sniff again. Suddenly he whipped about, lowered his head, and charged. I was getting pictures and I didn't realize as I watched the animal in the viewfinder how close he really was. Our guide, Finn, slammed the Land Rover into reverse and we went flying down the road backward while I hung out of the top hatch snapping pictures and the rhino tried to ram his horn through the radiator. Fortunately, the animal gave up the chase after just a few seconds; our wild backward ride lasted long enough for me.

Peering through a camera's viewfinder changes one's perspective and the proper sense of distance is lost. Below Poacher's Lookout in Tsavo West, I was photographing a cow rhino and her two-year-old calf—a ton of infant. Because they were fairly close, I was using the 250mm lens on my Hasselblad. The cow shuffled back and forth, making the usual fuss of a disturbed rhino. Suddenly she charged. With my eye at the viewfinder I began to record the action on film, and I shouted to Finn not to move the Land Rover. Disregarding my request, he floored the gas pedal. By then the cow's bulk filled the viewfinder and I realized that we hadn't started moving away until she was about thirty feet from us. She would have covered that in less than two seconds.

After relating experiences of this sort, I have been asked by acquaintances if I consider an unarmed photographic safari dangerous. Not very. Things get quite exciting at times, but we always seem to be in control of the situation.

It is said that a leopard, unlike a charging lion, is never bluffing when it threatens to attack. Supposedly, you must either kill the leopard or it will kill you. After my experience in Serengeti, I wonder if this is really so. I got within thirty feet of a big, beautiful female leopard in a thorn tree (an unlikely spot, for they usually favor yellow-fever trees). I was not particularly nervous about getting close to take pictures because

Left: Leopard gazes at camera from thorn tree in Serengeti. Below: Masai giraffes shove at each other in short, indecisive fight. Bottom: Burchell's zebra pauses near herd of wildebeest.

she was well-fed; she had a Thomson's gazelle buck hanging up in her larder. I came closer still. She was above me and in position to reach me with one jump. While I took pictures, her lips curled back in displeasure, her tail flicked, and a growl rumbled from her chest. But she did not leap. I think she was merely warning me.

I will concede that there is often *potential* danger in the African wilds and this, I suppose, was one of the factors that made my safari so exciting. However, one has an excellent defense in the knowledge and skill possessed by an experienced professional guide. In addition, there are certain obvious precautions to be taken. Since many dangerous species are on the prowl at night, we always kept a fire burning in front of our tent and a lighted lantern hanging from the ridgepole. And if we had to leave the tent we carried a light. This will usually cause animals to keep their distance, though of course nature does not offer guarantees. Even with the fire and the lanterns going, we could often hear the soft, coughing grunts of hunting lions not far off in the encircling darkness.

Although a light will ward off most predators, there are some animals that evidently have no fear of illumination at night. Fortunately, I learned this through an experience with a nonpredatory animal. One night an elephant ambled into camp and, evidently guided by the light, came right up to the tent and scooped the bread, butter, and sugar from the table under our tent

Big black-maned lion stalks through thick grass. Most prides rely chiefly on hunting prowess of females, but males sometimes join in kill.

fly. We sat quietly and watched. One does not argue with an elephant.

Most of Africa, contrary to romanticized descriptions, is not smothered in forest and jungle. In the part of the continent I visited, the altitude and limited rainfall combine to produce vast grasslands. There is a "small" rainy season in November and a "big" one in April and May. Drought is common during the other months. The long dry season means dust, and for the photographer this is a problem. To prevent damage to my equipment I carried it in watertight cases while passing through country where the humidity was virtually nil. I found that the heat was never strong enough to endanger my film, but of course I never left it in direct sunshine.

The light readings in East Africa average one to two stops higher than would be normal in the eastern United States, and I found it necessary to use my exposure meter frequently. Anyone contemplating a photographic safari should either be adept at using a meter, or must rely on the limited potential of an electric-eye camera.

In one area, where we were permitted to leave our vehicle, I used a blind in an attempt to photograph crocodiles feeding on a wildebeest which lay dead on a riverbank. The venture was unsuccessful, as I did not have time to wait for the reptiles to return after they slithered away in alarm at the initial intrusion. Later I was able to get my crocodile pictures simply by making a careful stalk. Each success of that kind whets the appetite of a hunter or a photographer.

The rising popularity of camera safaris may lighten the hunting pressure on African game, while providing young African nations with added revenue, some of which can be used for conservation. These nations are trying hard to safeguard their wildlife. In the parks, of course, game is protected, and elsewhere in East Africa hunting is strictly controlled by means of a system originally set up by the British. Large areas are divided into numbered blocks, and records are kept of the fluctuations of game populations in each block. The number of hunting permits issued depends on how much pressure a given block can stand.

The greatest problem, poaching, probably will not be solved as long as the average African is poor. You cannot teach conservation to a hungry man. Even the wildlife in the parks is not always safe from the poacher. Natives sell illegally killed game and game products for a tiny fraction of the ultimate black-market price.

Huntable numbers of rhinos now exist in only two sectors of Kenya. A man who wants a rhino trophy must reserve a hunting block one to two years in advance, his safari must last a minimum of thirty-five days, the men and supplies must be taken into the shooting area by packhorse or camel—no vehicles permitted—and a special $500 permit must be purchased in addition to a general hunting license.

The days of unlimited trophy hunting are about over. As a hunter myself, I do not suggest that the gun should be replaced by the camera, but I do support the idea of self-imposed limitation. While many a sportsman has never seen Africa, a surprisingly large number have gone on numerous safaris. The self-limitation proposal, which has gained many adherents, is that each hunter restrict himself to one great African trophy—lion, or elephant, or whatever—in his lifetime. Until he found his trophy of a lifetime, a man would reach for his camera instead of his gun, and afterward he would again shoot his animals with a camera. This would assure hunting for future generations. As a man who stalks dangerous animals with a Hasselblad, I can say that this approach to the sport does not lessen the adventure.

Photograph of New England sportsmen shows that occasionally dugouts were still used by anglers late in nineteenth century.

 CONTINUED FROM PAGE 34

reportedly was capable of carrying forty men on sea voyages as far as Massachusetts Bay.

Log dugouts were particularly well suited to the needs of the oyster fishery, being so employed along the Connecticut shore almost down to the present day. Two such pine oyster dugouts, approximately thirty feet long, still survive at Mystic Seaport.

To increase dugout capacity, their sides were sometimes built up by the addition of planks, or they might be split down the center lengthwise, so that planks could be inserted between the two sides.

Craft derived from Indian log dugouts attained their ultimate development, as sailing canoes, brogans, and bugeyes in the Chesapeake in the late nineteenth century. Somewhat more than a hundred years previous to this, the Rev. Robert Rose, rector of St. Ann's Parish in Albemarle, in the Virginia tidewater, is credited with the invention of a "tobacco boat" consisting of two large dugout canoes placed side by side and overlaid with a stout platform for transporting tobacco casks.

Curiously, a nearly exact duplicate of this craft crops up a century or so later on the upper Missouri for tranporting bales of furs downriver. Log dugouts were a principal means of transportation on the upper Missouri in the early years. Immense cottonwood trees found in the rich river bottoms provided logs as large as thirty feet long and two-and-a-half feet across. In hollowing these, thin transverse sections were sometimes left in to serve as bulkheads, producing several separate tight compartments. Shipments of wild honey were sent down to St. Louis in them, as well as bear's grease, which served as cooking fat in place of lard, since bears were more plentiful on the upper Missouri than hogs.

Besides log dugouts, now all but forgotten, birch canoes were employed in New England from earliest times. Hunters, woodsmen, and explorers borrowed the birch from the Indians, yet never adopted it for commercial transportation to the same extent as dugout craft, nor did the white settlers ever undertake to build bark canoes themselves.

One of the first accounts of the birchbark canoe in New England is by Martin Pring, who commanded the *Speedwell* from Bristol, England, when that vessel visited Plymouth Harbor seventeen years before the landing of the Pilgrims. "Their Boats, whereof we brought one to Bristoll, were in proportion like a wherrie of the River of Thames, seventeen foot long and four foot broad, made of Barke of a Birch-tree, farre exceeding in bigness those of England; it was sowed together with strong and tough Oziers or twigs, and the seams covered over with Rozen or a Turpentine little inferior in sweetness to Frankincense, as we made trial by burning a little thereof on coals at sundry times after our comming home; it was also open like a Wherrie, and sharp at both ends, saving that the beake was a little bending roundly upward. And though it carried nine men standing upright, yet it weighed not at the most above sixtie pounds."

Of all the Maine rivers the Penobscot is most noted for its canoes. At Old Town, above Bangor, canoes are still manufactured, although no longer of birchbark by Indians. Here at Indian Island (which, by the way, is still tribal territory and not a reservation) Henry David Thoreau engaged Joe Polis for a trip to Moosehead Lake and the Allegash in 1857. Joe, a wealthy Indian who lived in a fine white house and was reputed to be worth $6,000, a fortune acquired from moose hunting, agreed to go for a dollar and a half a day, and fifty cents a week extra for his canoe. Newly built by Polis himself, the canoe, according to Thoreau, was neatly and stanchly put together with stout ribs and extra-thick bark. It looked small to Thoreau for three men and 166 pounds of

dunnage, and getting out his ever-ready "black ash rule," Thoreau took its dimensions for the benefit of posterity: eighteen feet three inches long, two feet six inches at its greatest beam, and one foot deep amidships. Indeed, this canoe was somewhat smaller than a Penobscot River canoe still to be seen at the Peabody Museum of Salem, the oldest surviving birchbark canoe known, having been donated to the East India Marine Society in 1826.

The weight of Polis' canoe Thoreau estimated to have been about eighty pounds. In any case, Polis, who was stoutly built and slightly over middle height, evidently lugged it easily enough when required, sometimes on the run. And if it at first seemed small to Thoreau, it carried his party of three safely enough, even during very rough weather on Moosehead Lake.

The name Passamaquoddy, according to Frank Speck, means "Those whose occupation is pollock fishing." The Passamaquoddy, a Malecite tribe formerly occupying the valley of the St. Croix River and the shores at the mouth of the bay to which they have given their name, developed an ocean-going bark canoe of outstanding ability in rough water. The ends of the canoe were low to cut windage, and pointed, yet full enough for good lift. The raking stem and cutaway forefoot, together with the rising bottom rocker toward the ends, allowed the canoe to be swung quickly by a strong and skillful paddle to meet oncoming waves, to backwater, or to run down a breaking crest.

Not only did the Passamaquoddy take pollock in these bark canoes, but they were accustomed to going miles offshore at the mouth of the Bay of Fundy in all kinds of weather, winter and summer, to shoot porpoise. At one time the sale of porpoise oil was the chief source of income for this tribe. Two Indians commonly hunted together, one to steady the pitching canoe as best he could with the paddle, while the other stood up to throw the spear.

Beyond the territory once occupied by the

New Brunswick Malecite lies the ancient hunting range of the Micmac, extending from eastern New Brunswick across Nova Scotia to Newfoundland and the coast of Labrador. Micmac canoes were built in a number of models—light wood canoes for easy portaging, river canoes with rounded bottoms for fast paddling and running rapids—but most distinctive were the deep rough-water, or ocean-going, canoes, otherwise known as "humpbacks." The gunwales of these canoes rose amidships, producing a decided hump in the sheer at the center of the canoe, giving additional freeboard at the point where cresting waves were most apt to curl aboard when seas were running high.

In these humpbacks the Micmacs often ventured far to sea, porpoise hunting or on journeys. Canoes crossed from Digby to St. John, New Brunswick. Abram Toney, former chief of the Yarmouth Micmacs, once paddled as far as Grand Manan, and on another occasion claimed to have spent the night on a whistling buoy twenty-one miles off Yarmouth, having been caught offshore in his canoe by a sudden blow while porpoise hunting.

The Micmacs were not the only northeastern tribe to venture long distances at sea in birch canoes. Regularly each summer from time immemorial, the now extinct Beothuk Indians of Newfoundland visited the Funk Islands forty miles offshore by open sea from Cape Freels to fill their canoes with seafowl eggs which they dried in cake form to enrich their winter diet.

The materials used in constructing the Beothuk canoe were the usual ones, birchbark sewn and served with flexible spruce roots and sealed with tempered pitch, ribbed and reinforced with thin splits of spruce, substituting for cedar which does not grow in Newfoundland. But in its shape this unique canoe was unlike any other Indian craft. Its crescent profile was aptly likened by one early explorer to the "new moone." Its sheer line was in actuality two crescent arcs meeting in a peak amidships which stood nearly as high as the slim, upturned ends. In thwartships section the slightly curved sides opened upward in a narrow V, so that the canoe sat deep in the water and required ballast to keep it upright. Yet these canoes seem to have been excellent sea boats, both able and fast, and of ample capacity. It has been suggested that the influence of Norsemen, visiting America long before Columbus, may account for the odd shape of these vessels. The canoes bear some resemblance to small fishing boats used along the west coast of Norway for more than a thousand years.

Our modern canoes derive directly from the aboriginal birch canoes of the Algonquian-speaking tribes of northeastern America. These earliest migrants from Asia are believed to have come as sub-Arctic hunters across the wide land bridge now submerged under the Bering Strait, possibly thirty thousand years ago, or even earlier. Probably they did not bring canoes with them in any developed form, although birchbark canoes of an inferior sort occur in Siberia. Indeed, crude bark canoes in great variety are found throughout the world.

Not until the Algonquian tribes had crossed the continent and established themselves where the white men found them is it likely that the birchbark canoe was perfected. Nature put materials of superlative quality in one area only—that is to say, in the region extending south of Hudson Bay to the Great Lakes, thence east through the watershed of the St. Lawrence and its tributaries, and across northern New England and the Canadian Maritimes to the sea.

Here the canoe birch, or paper birch, sometimes attains a height of a hundred feet and a diameter of thirty inches or more at the butt. Its bark is one-eighth to three-six-

LEONARD LEE RUE III

Algonquian-style birchbark canoes are still built by a few Indian craftsmen, employing traditional methods, black-spruce servings, and white-cedar ribs.

LEONARD LEE RUE III

teenths of an inch thick. Not only is such bark tougher than any other but, being impregnated with natural oils, it neither absorbs water nor rots. To sew such bark and to bind it with servings about the gunwales and stems, the fibrous, flexible roots of the black spruce are ideal. These roots will be found in damp ground, close to the surface, under moss, sometimes as long as twenty feet, with a uniform diameter hardly larger than a lead pencil. Such roots were carefully prepared, split, and sometimes quartered, and kept damp to retain their original pliability. Melted spruce gum, expertly tempered with fat and powdered charcoal, produced excellent pitch for sealing.

The wood of large, clear, straight-grain, white-cedar butts was also essential. The wood of the northern white cedar is extremely lightweight, yet adequately tough and strong, as well as bendable. Straight-grain white cedar can be split, if one knows how, into thin, uniform strips. Other timber, in particular black spruce, can also be split, but not with equal precision and facility.

Even after the Indians acquired steel axes and crooked knives, building a canoe remained an extended and laborious operation, requiring numerous skills and specialized knowledge. Canoe birches of large size and superior bark were never plentiful. One might search for weeks before finding a suitable tree. Winter bark is the best, but getting it off the tree in one piece in the winter was a slow, precarious process best accomplished with hot water. Felling a large tree so that it might be more easily worked on presented difficulties, too, and there was the risk of damaging the bark. Cedar splits best when dry. Thus it was desirable to cut or girdle selected trees long enough in advance to permit seasoning. After the materials were assembled, an earthen building bed had to be formed and staked; gunwales cut and bent; bark shaped, cut, and sewed; nu-

Top: At meeting of canoe enthusiasts in 1880's, kayak-like decked canoes predominated. Above: Canoe shown at Lake George in 1881 had sun canopy. Right: American Canoe Association member W. M. Carter sails his racer, "Singara."

merous wooden parts worked to shape and size; and so on.

In the beginning, before trails had been chopped through the wilderness, one mighty, natural thoroughfare led into the heart of America—the St. Lawrence River, its tributaries, and connecting waterways. The river extends a distance of two thousand miles to Lake Nipigon, beyond Lake Superior, and drains some four hundred thousand square miles. This was Algonquian territory, canoe territory. In this vast region the birchbark canoe played out its final spectacular role. For more than two hundred years, fur-trade canoes hauled their annual cargoes of wilderness riches to Montreal. Well into the nineteenth century, the great birch canoes of the voyageurs continued to make their annual circuit from Montreal to Grand Portage at the height of land on the northern extremity of Lake Superior, and back again before the winter freeze-up.

Each year, when passage opened on the St. Lawrence through the spring ice, the canoe brigades set out, hundreds of huge canoes bound west, for *le pays d'en haut*. Brigade after brigade of big canoes, bright with color and gaily blazoned insignia, departed upriver in orderly formation. The red-shirted voyageurs in their tasseled stocking caps and fringed, varicolored sashes, flashed vermilion-tipped paddles, dipping vigorously to the rhythm of old French paddling songs.

Canoes of the largest size, *canots des maîtres*, ran to thirty-six feet in length, were manned by crews of fourteen, and needed four men on the portage. *Bâtards*, the slightly smaller version of the canots des maîtres, required a crew of twelve. On the lesser inland waters west of the Grand Portage were found the smaller North canoes, *canôts des nord*. Generally not more than twenty-five feet in length, these canoes were worked with crews of six to eight, and were easily carried by two men.

The brigades, starting west, soon turned aside from the rapids of the St. Lawrence to follow the more placid though indirect Ottawa, and as they advanced its brown waters finally grew shallower until paddles were changed for setting poles—long, slim, and iron-tipped—on which the voyageurs leaned and pushed, making slow headway against the flow. When they had passed Lake Nipissing and had carried over into the French River, paddling was resumed, and with the help of the current they came more easily down to Georgian Bay, the nearly separate upper portion of Lake Huron. The Jesuit missionary, Father Jean

Painter Frederic Remington is shown in cedar cruising canoe, using double-bladed paddle on St. Lawrence waters near his Ogdensburg home.

de Brebeuf, who came this way in the early seventeenth century, recorded that the passage included thirty-five portages, some six miles long, besides at least fifty places where all hands had to jump into the water to drag the canoes through shallows and rapids.

Having come to Georgian Bay, the canoes turned west, in time passing Mackinac Island, and eventually Sault Ste. Marie, continuing along the upper shore of Lake Superior to Grand Portage (later Fort William), at its northern extremity. Outside the palisades of the fort they might find a thousand Indians encamped. At this wilderness crossroads thousands assembled annually to pow-wow and trade.

According to one qualified witness, U.S. Boundary Commissioner Major Joseph Delafield, whose diary for 1823 survives, the French Canadian was a superior woodsman, more hardy than the Indian. The elite of the voyageurs were the *hivernants*, the "winterers." They lived the year around in the back country and were contemptuous of the ordinary voyageurs who returned to Montreal for the winter. But whether a canoeman wintered in the wilderness or not, he had to be incredibly tough.

There was not only paddling, but innumerable portages, as well. The paddlers jumped into rapid water up to their waists, armpits, or necks when necessary, to hold the canoe off the rocks until it could be unloaded. On the carry, two hundred pounds was accounted a fair load—two kegs of pork of ninety-six pounds each, or three bushels of corn weighing about as much. With such a load on his back tied to the two ends of a long strap, or tumpline, across his forehead, the bearer, leaning well forward and with knees slightly bent, was off at a fast walk or slow trot. Usually it was necessary to return several times before everything had been carried across.

Voyageurs had to be tough for other reasons. Unbridled competition between fur companies resulted in ambuscades at carrying places, and bloody encounters in the woods. This did not end until 1821, when the North West Company was absorbed by Hudson's Bay Company. One result was an end to the fighting. Another was the replacement of fur-trade canoes by Hudson's Bay boats, which by then had proved to be more economical and serviceable.

The birchbark canoe declined with the aboriginal Indian. Such craft were never built by whites, and were used less and less by them as the nineteenth century advanced. Even before 1840, white trappers and market hunters in the Adirondack wilderness had adopted crude precursors of the celebrated guide-boat.

The open canoe, managed with the single-bladed paddle and modeled on the birch, but constructed of other materials, achieved only limited popularity before 1900. About that time, however, the demand for the open, canvas-covered canoe jumped quite spectacularly. Meanwhile, for the three previous decades quite a different canoe held the center of the stage. This was a small decked-over craft resembling the Eskimo kayak more than it did the Indian birch, and lightly planked with wood, usually varnished white cedar. Most of these were fitted for sailing, often with intricate rigs. Otherwise they were propelled with the double-bladed paddle. Originated for cruising, they were sailed more than they were paddled, and evolved rather quickly into ever more specialized racing machines.

It all started with John MacGregor, a British missionary, sportsman, author, and lecturer, who visited North America in 1859. He tried canoes, presumably the birch, on the Ottawa River, and continuing across the continent experimented with Eskimo kayaks in the Arctic. Returning to Britain, MacGregor built his first fourteen-foot Rob Roy

cruising canoe on the kayak idea, but planked like a boat with wood. It weighed about seventy pounds. In this canoe and in succeeding Rob Roys, MacGregor cruised through the British Isles and a great part of Europe, eventually going as far afield as Scandinavia and the Holy Land. As a popular writer and lecturer, MacGregor converted Britain to the gospel of the cruising canoe. His most famous book, *A Thousand Miles in the Rob Roy Canoe on Twenty Rivers and Lakes of Europe*, was first published in 1866, the same year the Royal Canoe Club was founded in London.

America was ready to follow suit. A new urban class with increasing leisure and means had begun to turn to nature and to sports for recreation. In 1871 the New York Canoe Club, modeled after the Royal Canoe Club, came into being with sixteen members, each of whom had a sailing canoe.

Canoeing received some marvelous publicity. In 1874, Nathaniel Holmes Bishop paddled his *Maria Theresa*, a fifteen-foot paper canoe made by the Waters Paper Boat Company of Troy, New York, all the way from that city down the Hudson and the length of the Atlantic coast to Florida. His book, *The Voyage of the Paper Canoe*, was an immediate best-seller.

In 1879 three cruising enthusiasts reached Elk Lake at the source of the Mississippi with Rob Roy canoes. Two years later another canoeist-explorer returned from the headwaters of the same river to paddle from Aitkin, Minnesota, to the Gulf of Mexico, according to his claim, a distance of 3,184 miles in one hundred and seventeen days. Even longer was the five-month cruise of Charles A. Neidé in the *Aurora*, a Rushton Princess canoe, in the company of his friend Captain Samuel D. Kendall in a home-made canoe, *Solid Comfort*. They traveled from Lake George in the Adirondacks to the Gulf of Mexico.

J. Henry Rushton, born and raised in northern New York at the edge of the Adirondack wilderness, was the foremost American canoe-maker of this period. He helped to found the American Canoe Association in 1880, and he became world-famous for his Rob Roy and Indian Girl models in both lapstrake and "smoothskin" versions. His canoes more or less followed the contours of the aboriginal birchbarks but with refinements and were constructed entirely of cedar. (Some late Rushton models were canvas-covered in deference to the public's changing tastes.) He and a few fellow-craftsmen were chiefly responsible for the resurgence of the classic canoe which remains in use today.

A cedar canoe that came from the Rushton Boat Shop in Canton, New York, circa 1912, is now in the possession of Atwood Manley, author of *Rushton and His Times in American Canoeing* (published jointly by the Adirondack Museum and Syracuse University Press in 1968). Manley's Rushton is a fifteen-footer named *Vayu*—for the Hindu god of the winds—and is still perfectly stanch. Its owner was caught in it by a nasty gale in 1967 on Blue Mountain Lake. "There were three-foot waves," he recalls, "but my little canoe rode them like a duck."

The Rushtons were light, maneuverable, graceful, seaworthy, and very durable. Probably the lightest craft ever cruised in successfully were the five pint-sized lapstrake cedar canoes Rushton built for the diminutive and sickly woodsman-author, George Washington Sears, who signed his many contributions to *Forest and Stream*, Nessmuk. *Wood Drake*, the first of the Nessmuk miniatures, measured ten feet and weighed but fifteen pounds, nine-and-one-half ounces before painting, which added another two pounds. She carried her owner dry and safe over Adirondack waterways in the summer of 1880. The smallest and most remarkable of the five was *Sairy Gamp* (which never took water), weighing ten-and-a-half pounds for her nine-foot length. Her builder was afraid she might crack apart like an egg shell, but after a successful six-week cruise Nessmuk pronounced her dry and safe, and as good as new. After many years at the Smithsonian Institution, the *Sairy Gamp* is now on display at the Adirondack Museum.

As the racing fad subsided, and with it the sailing canoe, the open paddling canoe—today's basic design—grew ever more popular. Its form continued to recapitulate the Indian birch except for a watertight covering of painted canvas over a wooden hull. Rushton would have much preferred to go on building the beautiful varnished all-wood cedar canoes for which he was—and still remains—famous, but he was a businessman and he did what had to be done to save his business. The public was demanding canvas-covered paddling canoes. After designing his canvas-covered Indian models, in 1902 he turned over production to an experienced canoe-builder brought in from the Penobscot River where the Indians had been building superior birchbarks for countless generations. Thousands of canvas canoes were built and sold, keeping the shop open during the last years of Rushton's life.

Since then, the paddling canoe has had its ups and downs. For a time competition with the automobile as well as the outboard motor cut into the demand for canoes. But more recently canoes have come back strong and continue to gain. During the last couple of decades, wood-and-canvas construction has given way to aluminum, plastic, and hardened rubber, yet the basic design remains constant. Though aluminum has the drawbacks of being noisy and taking dents, it is obviously durable and requires minimal maintenance—no calking, painting, or varnishing. Moreover, an aluminum canoe does not easily swamp. Fiberglass is heavier than aluminum, but just about as durable, and hardened latex has the same advantages with a little less weight. To repair the canvas covering of an old canoe, one needs Ambroid glue, unbleached muslin patches, and sandpaper to roughen the edges for a good bond. A small rip or puncture in an aluminum canoe can be quickly repaired with nothing more than a tube of liquid solder, and there are tough, fast-setting epoxy-resin glues for plastic and latex craft. Modern canoes are so maneuverable, stable on the water, and easily repaired that they remain the best means of travel on remote waterways.

Despite the variety of materials and models now available, all are close copies of the original Indian birch. Increasing numbers of campers and sportsmen are turning to canoes. Longer vacations, earlier retirement, and the general movement away from polluted cities and off congested and deadly highways combine to swell the demand. There is still a primeval wilderness in the North to escape to, and nothing quite equals the paddling canoe to enjoy it in. ⊙

after he is gone. There have always been men to whom it is important to remember.

Henry William Herbert, grandson of the first Earl of Carnarvon, came to New York as a "remittance man," a British euphemism for a member of the family more comfortable to have far from home. Under the pseudonym Frank Forester, he wrote of shooting in New York State, particularly near Warwick, from 1831 until his suicide in 1858 at the age of fifty-one. His writing and his shooting life were colorful, with touches like making the trip up from New York in a four-in-hand coach. Some of his most interesting reminiscences, classics of the gun-diary genre, are in *The Warwick Woodlands*, *My Shooting Box*, *American Game in its Seasons*, *Field Sports of the U. S. & British Provinces of North America*, *Sporting Scenes and Characters*.

I had access to the gun diary of the late Dr. Charles C. Norris of Bryn Mawr, Pennsylvania, which he kept from July 22, 1893, through his last day's shooting on November 10, 1959, with entries like these:

DATE	LOCALITY	GAME	NOTES
1/8 1898	*Huntley, Md.*	*1 goose 2 dippers 1 blk. duck 9 quail 5 jacksnipe*	*With W.B.C. (Dr. Cadwalader). Bay frozen in first fine day.*
11/9 1898	*York Co., New Brunswick*	*1 bull moose, 50 in.*	*Lynford Biddle got a small moose. I missed a caribou.*
12/23-27 1906	*Rutherfordton, N. C.*	*15 quail*	*Shot 1 day, 2 half days.*
10/26 1938	*Yarmouth, Nova Scotia*	*8 'cock 1 grouse*	*One 'cock missed, 10 shells used.*

My friend Bob Wingard writes of shooting from a Susquehanna River "roll-over" duck boat:

"A day we had given up on, proved one we never forgot. It was October 25, 1949, 50°, intermittent rain, north wind shifting to northeast. Many ducks flew but the wind seemed to be urging them on to the bay. We had little shooting though the list of ducks was impressive: baldpates, pintails, redheads, blacks, mallards, green-winged teal, canvasbacks, goldeneyes, buffleheads, scaup, ring-necked duck, and Canada geese.

"In late afternoon a straggling line of geese came down the river sounding like a pack of barking hounds. Biff grabbed his call which hadn't turned a head all day on the high-flying V's, but these birds were tired. They turned, broke line, and a dozen or so hooked wings and set in about a mile downriver. Thirty or forty landed a quarter mile below us among patches of three-square bulrush and rock ledges. I found a channel and was starting to push them together when a pair we hadn't noticed raised their long necks from the edge of some three-square directly in front and open to the boat. As they jumped, the rest followed them into the wind. What a sight and sound as that wall of Canadas rose toward us. Biff made two clean kills."

In his reminiscences, Henry Herbert stresses what many early gunners seemed concerned with—the large bags that could be taken. Bob Wingard puts you on a river you may never have seen, gives you the clamor of wings and the stimulation of the day without his having fired a shot.

A gun diary is possibly the most revealing part of a shooting man anyone will see. I regret that my father and grandfather didn't keep them, for they would be an enviable legacy. It would be especially interesting if someone were to leave a complete gun diary now, to be opened a hundred years

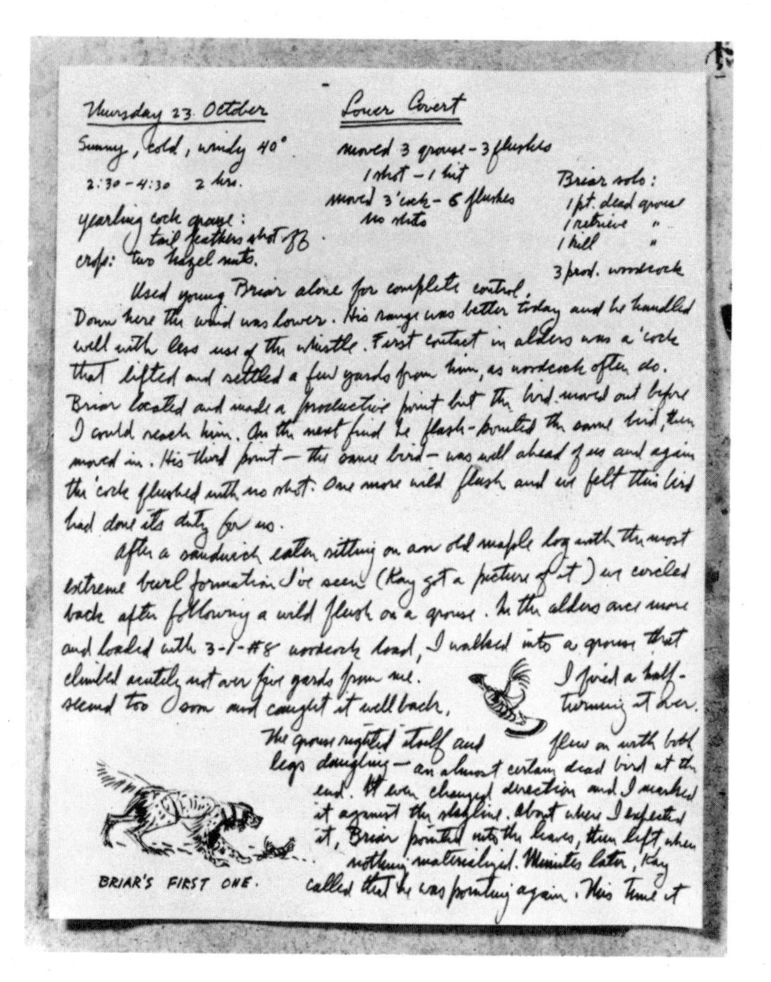

Thursday 23 October — Lower Covert

Sunny, cold, windy 40°
2:30–4:30 2 hrs.

moved 3 grouse – 3 flushes
1 shot – 1 hit
moved 3 'cock – 6 flushes
no shots

Briar solo:
1 pt. dead grouse
1 retrieve "
1 kill "
3 prod. woodcock

yearling cock grouse:
tail feathers shot off.
crop: two hazel nuts.

Used young Briar alone for complete control. Down here the wind was lower. His range was better today and he handled well with less use of the whistle. First contact in alders was a 'cock that lifted and settled a few yards from him, as woodcock often do. Briar located and made a productive point but the bird moved out before I could reach him. On the next find he flash-pointed the same bird, then moved in. His third point — the same bird — was well ahead of us and again the 'cock flushed with no shot. One more wild flush and we felt this bird had done its duty for us.

After a sandwich eaten sitting on an old maple log with the most extreme burl formation I've seen (Kay got a picture of it) we circled back after following a wild flush on a grouse. In the alders once more and loaded with 3-1-#8 woodcock load, I walked into a grouse that climbed acutely not over five yards from me. I fired a half-second too soon and caught it well back, turning it over. The grouse righted itself and flew on with both legs dangling — an almost certain dead bird at the end. It even changed direction and I marked it against the skyline. About where I expected it, Briar pointed into the leaves, then left when nothing materialized. Minutes later, Kay called that he was pointing again. This time it

later, picturing what shooting was like "back in 1970."

I began my shooting notes in 1932 as a record of hits and misses, the number of birds moved, with mention of weather. I tried to capture a few experiences that make a day special, and later added rough pen sketches—some indicating where I fired as I swung through the bird. I soon felt the need to credit productive points and retrieves of each dog. In 1952 I started noting the sex of each grouse shot, its markings, crop contents, and whether the bird was adult or juvenile. I now record the age and sex of all woodcock and pheasants shot.

A gun diary can be as elaborate as the gunner cares to make it. My notes are on loose pages, grouped by seasons. Not all the entries are exceptional, not all are happy, for there are those empty places after a dog has gone. But in those pages there are more than a thousand days in the field shared with my dogs, and I know they asked no more. There is that first season after the war, back home in our mountains and the glory of October; a comment in 1951: "Old Blue spent this season by the fire, confining his record to birds-sniffed-at-the-door." There is a sketch of Ruff pointing stanchly; a drawing of Dixie as a puppy wading downstream to keep even with a drink.

Beyond the color of memorable days, a gun diary can be an important record of shooting averages, of loads used, of a dog's performance and progress, the number of days you have hunted, how certain coverts have produced, the name of a landowner from whom you may want permission to hunt years later.

I may cling to the idea of a Glorious Twenty-fifth—an auspicious date in October when woodcock flights frequently arrive—but in seasons when this fails to materialize, my notes are valuable in reminding me of how erratic the flights have been. There was the season following an abnormally dry summer:

WEDNESDAY 16 OCTOBER 1963, DOLLY SODS

Hot, dry, overcast, 78°

Moved 21 'cock—25 flushes,
8 shots—4 hits

SHADOWS:	DIXIE:
2 productives	*7 productives*
5 backs	*2 backs*
4 kills	*4 kills*
3 retrieves	*1 retrieve*

"After the drought the low coverts are baked too hard for woodcock and no flight birds have appeared. Recalling a day when fog caught us in these highlands with woodcock dropping in the vapor, Kay and I tried it today on chance that frequent fogs that hover here at near-4,000 feet have kept the soil damp. Drove north past one-sided wind-

Left: Typical page of gunning diary describes performance of promising young setter. Below and on subsequent pages are sketches from diary.

blown spruce and fiery mountain-ash berries, with beaver ponds like broken mirrors in swamps that sprawl to the west.

"At Blackbird Knob Trail I let Shadows and Dixie out while I assembled the little Purdey, and Shadows ran downwind into a woodcock that topped the brush and disappeared like a cork on flood water. Walking barrens like Scottish moorland, my optimism faded. In clear light without fog and the whistle of wings this looked unpromising. Then Kay called, 'There goes one.'

"It had been in a miserable clump of stunted alders near a spring seep. Dixie took the line of flight and soon she and Shadows hit scent. Dixie stiffened and Shadows backed, and this time the bird gave me a low skimming flush and dropped obligingly out of a puff of feathers. Shadows retrieved—a yearling male.

"We worked to a tributary of Red Creek flowing through soil damp enough to show one turkey track the width of my spread fingers. There were hoary alders downstream but no cattle to enhance it as woodcock cover. From outside, I heard Dixie's bell go silent and a moment later the deeper tone of Shadow's sleigh bell abruptly ceased. Pushing my way backwards to spring the alder stems and keep both hands on the gun, I could hear Kay's movie camera buzzing. If, as old-timers say, woodcock go for the light, this one was going to have rough flushing. Watching the dogs, I took one more step and heard it twitter up, saw a form against a tiny piece of sky, fired, and heard Kay call, 'You dropped it!' Dixie made the retrieve.

"Back in the open, we paused for a sandwich. I took out my first bird and laid it beside the warm one on my lap. 'Even in that light I knew this one was a hen.' I stretched the wings and examined the underside of the secondaries. 'An adult,' I said.

"'You knew two flushed on that point?' Kay asked. I hadn't.

"We came to clumps of aspen with whitewash splashings on fallen tobacco-brown heart-shaped leaves that a few weeks ago had been the color of newly minted gold. Plastered to black earth with moisture of countless fogs, they gave off tannic pungency when kicked. There were those little St.-John's-wort leaves that resemble woodcock tail feathers—a good omen. To prove it, Dixie went on point. I missed the 'cock as it squirmed up and around the silvery aspen trunks. As I ejected the empty shell, two more went up in front of the still-steady Dixie. With a loaded left barrel I stood with my mouth as open as the gun and watched them disappear.

"With this many birds, I set myself a limitation of shots over points only—not the easiest. If, as some damned fool said, you should never miss a woodcock, I'll say you shouldn't miss too many with both barrels—which I did on the next point. I think there's no miss that makes you feel so silly.

"A trek over a stretch of bare rocks

brought us in sight of the station wagon toward sunset. Woodcock produce action to the last minute and we moved a number in the final cover. The last kill was over a point and the bird fell in dense alders that seemed an improbable place to find a stone-dead 'cock but after several minutes Shadows wriggled his way back out and delivered the bird with a wide grin. I gave him the pat he was waiting for.

"Driving back along the Forest Service Road, the far black-purple mountains looked like clouds with spruce edgings against the red afterburn of sunset. It had been an exceptional day but several things suggest more than coincidence: 1) dry conditions in low coverts, offset by fogs up here, provided ideal conditions to send the woodcock to highlands; 2) the gap at Blackbird Knob Trail draws migrating songbirds—bird-banders use this area—and may have same attraction for flight woodcock; 3) this high-country—spruce swamps, tundra with beaver ponds and alders—may attract 'cock because it resembles breeding grounds in Canada.

"We paused to look east toward Shenandoah Mountain and Virginia. A woodcock came out of nowhere from behind the car and flickered into the south, its long bill pointing down in that urgent attitude of motion. The dusking flight had started."

Reading a 1954 entry, I detected symptoms that led to the discovery that I'd been shooting for twenty-seven years with a gun-stock that didn't fit me, a revelation that ended happily with a custom restocking job. It began innocuously enough on a pheasant shoot in New Jersey:

TUESDAY 26 OCTOBER 1954, AMWELL PRESERVE
Hot, flaming color, 70°, 3 hrs.
Moved 13 to 15 pheasants
15 shots—3 hits

RUFF:	FEATHERS:
several productives	*several productives*
1 retrieve	*2 retrieves*

"We'd used our dogs on pheasants for training but I had never shot at one up to now. After nearly thirty years of grouse shooting I was looking forward to two days of this new kind of gunning, and our host, Dr. Charles Norris, had assured me that after grouse I probably wouldn't miss a bird. This should have put me on guard.

"Dr. Norris was shooting one half of the preserve, I the other with Duncan Dunn as my guide. Kay had a new movie camera, Ruff and Feathers were quartering out ahead, and everything was set for pheasants to begin falling. We weren't out of sight of the cars when between the dogs and me a big cock pheasant flared up like a chunk of the scarlet-and-gold foliage and leveled off. I can't remember ever seeing so much open space or a slower bird. I even turned to Dunn and inquired. 'All right to shoot here?' and at his nod, swung past the bird and fired. The damned thing ignored me so I swung through again, found myself too far ahead and stopped my barrels before shooting, and missed again. The embarrassing part was watching the pheasant laze out of sight for five seconds longer. Kay got it all on film, with the back of my neck turning fiery red.

"My next chance was in a small thickly-grown draw and the bird came back low over my head. I turned and fired and saw it go down fluttering—and learned what a wing-broken pheasant can do. We regretfully gave up and moved into a strip of corn. A moment after Feathers showed indication of game, a hen flushed well out, crossing right. Feeling a need for power to bring one of these birds down, I fired my choke barrel, missed, and then dropped the bird far out with the modified right. Feathers delivered nicely—a bird with lovely restrained tans and violet overtones.

"With a bit more confidence I approached a fine point by Feathers in an isolated clump of cover. The bird lay nicely, then came straight up from between my boots and climbed for the sky. I turned and tried to take it going away, almost shooting vertically, and wondered if there'd been any shot in the two empties I ejected.

"There were some wild flushes and several points by Ruff and the birds seemed so slow and I seemed so futile. After an unproductive period we made a wide cast to another corner of the preserve and I welcomed the lull and almost dreaded another flush. I finally dropped another bird—a cock that appeared to be going a little faster than the others, which helped.

"On our way back we took the little draw where I'd lost the cock pheasant and, part way through, Kay called that Feathers was on point. As I moved to him I saw him with my wounded bird in his mouth. Even then, it struggled free but he caught it and held it firmly until I arrived."

Though I fired fifteen shells to drop only three pheasants that day, it is the memory of those two pieces of air I blasted from around that first cock pheasant that can still, in the quiet of the night, make me break into a sweat. I later diagnosed the misfit in my gunstock—at least an alibi—but anyone who tells me you can't miss a pheasant isn't talking to the right man.

Statistics are significant when they are personal. Reading my older entries, it is astonishing how many things were different from the way I remembered them. With the present lows in grouse, it is difficult to realize that in '55 and '56 it wasn't unusual to move sixteen to twenty separate grouse in a half day in our Alleghenies.

Each season I keep a list of the coverts I hunt, and after the name of each covert I record the number of birds moved there, number of flushes, and the number shot. This gives at a glance the birds any covert has contained for comparison in different years; it also serves as an index for my detailed notes in the diary. For the gunner who doesn't have time to keep more than data, this alone makes an effective log, especially if he includes a record of hits and misses.

Shooting averages—the percentage of hits to shots—are accurate only if you count every shell fired. Such a record shows how quickly a nice average for one or two lucky days is reduced by the overall proportion of misses to hits. To analyze my shooting on ruffed grouse, my most difficult bird, I keep a page with a column on the left describing the angle of the shot, with entries of hits (●) and misses (o) for each season:

QUARTERING LEFT	1965	1966	1967
normal	● ● o o	● o	● ●
low	● ● o o o	● o	● ● o
rising	● ● ●	● o o o	
rising acutely	o		o
high	o	o	
overhead		o	
from tree	● o	●	

There are similar groups for quartering right, crossing left, crossing right, straightaway, away-left, away-right, incoming, incoming-left, incoming-right—altogether about seventy variations, and still there are shots difficult to classify. Comparing this with loads used in certain guns reveals what I am doing without guesswork.

In the quartering-left angle shots recorded above, I seemed to be doing better with rising shots in '65 than in '66; poorly on rising acutely and high shots; not badly on normal and low shots; rather well, for me, on out-of-tree shots; and, overall, a 48.5 percentage of hits, above average for me on grouse.

At the end of each year I summarize the season in this manner:

1966
56 days hunted. 36 coverts.
232 grouse moved—444 flushes.
6.44 bird/covert ratio.
Grouse:
60 shots—18 hits (30%).
Woodcock:
34 shots—20 hits (58.8%).
BLISS:
56 days hunted.
Grouse:
77 productives, 1 backpoint.
18 kills (6 over points).
16 retrieves.
Woodcock:
27 productives, 4 backpoints.
20 kills (all over points).
13 retrieves.

There are similar entries for each dog, with a running lifetime record.

A gun diary can reveal fluctuations of game populations, but it must be viewed as personal experience; to apply limited samplings to broad areas may magnify error.

The flush-per-hour count is not an accurate count of birds present. With a good dog I may find and flush the same grouse as many as five times in an hour, giving a five flush count; if I shoot that bird on the first flush I have a one flush-per-hour count—both counts possible with the same single bird. This is equally true with pheasants and woodcock. The more men in the party, the greater the probable flush count without putting any more birds in the covert than if one man were counting. Quail populations may be reflected in covey counts, provided someone doesn't count them over again the next day—a weakness in any state-wide hunter report on any game.

Drumming-counts on grouse and singing-counts on woodcock may be inflated, for a drumming grouse or a singing woodcock often performs in several places and may be counted as more than one. These methods account for only male birds and, unless you think optimistically that there is a girl for every boy, they are only educated guesses. Summer brood counts frequently have no direct relation to fall bird populations. Kill counts are realistic just so far as they reflect game taken, not game present. Whether a group of men are good or poor shots does not assess the number of birds present. If expert shots work a covert to the bone, a high kill report may signify that there are few, if any, birds left to breed; conversely, I've known men who could be in a bird population explosion and fail to hit one. An increased kill count may reflect an increased number of hunters, not more birds.

Acknowledging that any census method has shortcomings, a gun diary can still show the man who keeps it what he has been encountering in game numbers. It is more accurate than relying on one's memory, and consistent in that it is a single man making the observations without the vari-

able of several viewpoints. Over the seasons my notes have revealed a ratio that closely reflects ruffed grouse populations. Gunning a large number of coverts, each from one to four times per season, I keep a conservative count of separate grouse moved. Repeat visits to a covert do not affect the result, for any birds moved on former visits that season are discounted on later hunts. The number of grouse moved, divided by the number of coverts, gives a bird/covert ratio. In 1948 I moved 150 separate grouse in 23 coverts, or 6.52 per covert. The following season I again shot in 23 coverts, many of them the same as in '48, but I moved 207 grouse, giving a bird/covert ratio of 9.0. Any season averaging 6.0 grouse per covert has been a fair year. There have been years when this ratio was as low as 3.0, some years as high as 11.38.

The bird/covert ratio has its weaknesses—it is possible to gun a covert only once under adverse conditions and not move all the birds it holds; and it is not accurate if you hunt only a few coverts that hold an abnormally high number of birds. Since my shooting includes a comparable number of one-visit hunts every season and since I spread my shooting over a large section of the Alleghenies, the ratio as I find it is as balanced as personal experience will permit.

No grouse gunner doubts that ruffed grouse populations fluctuate, but if he divides the years into groups of ten (adhering to a popular notion about cycles) he is not likely to be able to forecast his chances for a given season. My diary shows that grouse populations where I have gunned have not followed a ten-year cycle or any other fixed pattern. Nor has there been any relation of high or low populations to wet or dry brood seasons the previous spring when compared with U. S. Climatological Reports. Woodcock populations appear more stable than grouse, but weather can affect op-

portunities to find them. Game population trends, or lack of them, as revealed in your gun diary are worthwhile if only to avoid cluttering your thinking with non-facts that have become almost traditional.

Crop-content records of pheasants and grouse and quail are enlightening and frequently surprising when kept for a long period. The effects of weather on the behavior of game and on the performance of your dog will give you an insight into ideal conditions for hunting. But even more important to me than records and conclusions about the birds I shoot, there are the dogs I shoot them over. Certain days glow like a sifting of golden maple leaves in an old lane in October, moments uncovered as I turn a page spotted with gun oil: the first season of each youngster I have started, a precious thing to go back to through the years as he develops; a feathered form laid in my hand, and setter eyes that seemed to say, *Did I do it right?*—described without knowing that next year she would be gone; mention of a sun that sank behind a purple ridge as I trudged that last mile to the station wagon with an empty game pocket, bone-tired as my dog, but immeasurably happy. For as long as I have my gun diary, many of the pages yellowed and beginning to smell of time, my setters will range the fall and winter woods. And for just as long, I'll be there.

whole area at a glance. Many are the mornings I went there for no other purpose than to watch fish crossing the bright sand like small shadows crossing the sun. I would leave my bike at the end of the road, take a path through a field where cows were grazing in a ghostly forest of dead cedar trees (the result of some massive blight), and eventually come to land's end on a ledge of rock thirty feet above the sea.

If no bonefish were in sight, usually a swarm of mullet would be there, circling madly in the shallows, or a few sullen old barracuda poised for trouble. It was even possible from time to time to make out the shapes of squid hovering just beneath the surface. And once, I remember, a school of jack blew across the scene, churning up the water like a passing rain squall. Why the sea chose this particular spot to dump such a spectacular pile of sand I am unable to say, but if you were to construct the ideal bonefishing flat, here would be the model.

That is why bonefishing at Whale Bay was the Mount Everest of fishing as far as I was concerned, and having scaled its dizzy heights, my head spinning in the rarefied air, I looked down with scorn upon the poor trudgers who occupied the lower elevations. Pompano fishermen, who sometimes appeared on the beach, I was able to tolerate. But whenever a charter boat came into view I recall that my sneers became snarls, for I visualized it as carrying to sea, along with tubs of cold beer, people whooping it up, who didn't know a marlin from a mackerel, and if they noticed the outriggers at all probably thought they were TV antennae.

Such is the snobbery bonefishing often leads to, especially in the early stages, and the reason I think of it now is because I recently returned to Bermuda after an absence of five years and caught a glimpse of Whale Bay from one of the boats I used to find so contemptible. In the interim Whale Bay had changed less than I had. True, there were houses standing where once there had been only trees, but the sand was still there, and so were the cliffs, and so were the birds flying about the cliffs like scraps of white paper blowing in the wind. One of the things I had discovered during the time I had been away was that the world does offer more than one kind of fishing worthy of the name, and that some of that fishing can be found in Bermuda. That was why I came back. Hitherto I had confined myself to the shallows of the island. Now I would find out what the depths had to offer.

Shaped like a fishhook, Bermuda is the summit of an immense mountain whose origins were almost certainly volcanic, and according to Robert W. Sayles, author of *Bermuda During the Ice Age*, the shape of the island "suggests that the volcano had at least two vents aligned in a northeast-southwest direction. The Challenger and Argus Banks lie on a similar trend line and are the eroded stumps of two volcanoes. At some time in the past, therefore, Bermuda was the site of a line of volcanoes." Between the island and the Banks the ocean is a mile deep, too deep for fishing. But once you reach the Banks, the first of which is Challenger, lying about fifteen miles southwest of Somerset, you enter one of the world's great fishing grounds. Here, as on Argus, some ten miles farther south, strong upwellings drive bait fish up the slopes and onto the top of the dead volcano where the water is only thirty fathoms deep and where marlin, wahoo, and blackfin and Allison tuna, all great game fish, gather to feed on them. In other words, the Banks are like two tables loaded with food which the ocean has laid close to Bermuda—a gigantic feast and one which lasts pretty much throughout the year, although the pickings are best from May through November.

I went in mid-September, when the

Blackfin tuna is brought aboard. Since marlin feed on this species, billfish may be encountered in any waters abounding with blackfin.

wahoo were gathering, in a boat called the *Coral Sea*, a 38-foot fishing machine built by the same hands that operated it, the hands of Boyd and Ted Gibbons, two blond and sun-scorched brothers from Ely's Harbour. When you step from land into a modern offshore fishing craft, you enter the age of technology afloat.

In our glistening twentieth-century ark we made our way swiftly to sea. Above the chasm between Bermuda and the Banks the color of the water was a deep midnight blue, but over the Banks it grew lighter. Sitting on the flying bridge, a windy perch above the hum of the diesel, I asked Boyd Gibbons what he thought about wahoo.

"He is some kind of a villain to get on a hook. I'll say that for him."

Boyd Gibbons' theory of why wahoo are harder than other fish to hook is based upon exploratory operations he has performed upon their stomachs. Like some other fish in the sea, a wahoo—a member of the mackerel family, long, slender, and incredibly swift—is a true cannibal: The wahoo eats its own kind. But what is unusual is that more often than not its victims' tails are missing.

There can be only one explanation for this, Boyd said. "A wahoo, when he is feeding, goes after fish from the rear. He cuts off their tails to immobilize them. Only then does he swing back around and swallow them head-on. That's why wahoo are hard as hell to hook. We call it tail trimming. They cut off the tail of your bait and leave the rest. Most wahoo are lost the instant they strike, because you can't get a hook into them."

By this time distance had reduced Bermuda to a small hump of land at the base of towering white clouds, "the remote Bermudas.../In th' Oceans...unespy'd"; it is easy to understand how this little fragment of coral and limestone, rising out of nowhere, once inspired such wonder among mariners. It was a marvelous morning. The sea had a bright spring to it, and whitecaps were scrawled across the surface—a good sea for wahoo, Boyd noted. Through a square of plate glass fixed into the floor at his feet, he could look down onto the depth finder in the cabin below us, and when the flickering red light told him we had reached the edge of Argus Bank, he slowed the boat, and baits were let out off the stern.

We were fishing four lines, two from the outriggers a couple of hundred feet behind the boat and two flat lines which were trolled from the stern between fifty and seventy-five feet back. Baits were mullet, flying fish, feathers, and a contraption Ted Gibbons calls his "enticer," a foot-long tube of wood with metal bands wrapped around it and a hook screwed into the rear. Fished close to the boat, it made wild, darting, erratic movements designed to bring fish in for a closer look. Teeth marks on the body indicated that at some time or other it had done just that.

Since all game fish are attracted to a moving bait, in waters like these, which accommodate many varieties of fish, it often turns out that although your mind is set on one kind of fish, you have to settle for something else. Our first fish of the day was a blackfin tuna which struck one of the flat lines soon after they were put out. It was a small tuna to begin with and grew smaller still before it reached the boat, thanks to an enormous barracuda which appeared upon the scene and began to tear chunks of flesh from the tuna's mid-section. It was really an appalling spectacle. By the time we were able to get what was left of the tuna out of the water, the barracuda had gorged itself into such a state of frenzy, boiling about the boat, that it swallowed one of the outrigger baits, both of which had been hauled in close to the boat when the tuna struck. After a short tussle we brought it to gaff and killed it. Of the tuna all that remained was a mangled head.

Unlike Allison tuna, a wahoo will run sideways when it is hooked, not down. Tuna rely on weight and depth to free themselves. A wahoo, like a bonefish, relies on speed, crackling through the water. Consequently, to fully appreciate them one should be holding the rod in his hand when the strike occurs, but since all of our wahoo were taken on outrigger baits (always the same outrigger, oddly enough, on the starboard side of the boat), I was denied that pleasure.

Both Allison and blackfin tuna are members of the mackerel family, just as the wahoo is. Although the Allison—or yellowfin tuna, as it is sometimes called—is occasionally difficult to tell from a blackfin or bigeye tuna, it is more brilliantly colored than these close relatives. The lower sides display white spots and vertical streaks, while there is a vague stripe of golden yellow on its upper sides and, as the name indicates, much bright yellow on the fins. The various tunas have been likened to torpedoes and even cigars in shape (which seems odd when one considers the pointed head, swept-back fins, and narrowly streamlined area between the thick body and the tail). But the fact is that all of these fish are graceful, powerful swimmers, capable of stripping line to great depths and doggedly resisting capture. Whereas a yellowfin tuna may weigh anywhere from twenty pounds to six times that much, the blackfin is relatively small—the average weight is less than ten pounds, though an occasional thirty-pounder is brought in.

Part of the excitement of fishing the Bermuda waters is the impossibility of foretelling what species, large or small, will strike. Of course, some species such as the white and blue marlins prefer surface-trolled baits, while others favor deeper presentations; but all of the game species will occasionally break the rules. Now and then an acrobatic white marlin may run to eighty pounds or a little more, while a blue may weigh three hundred. (And since blackfin tuna are a staple of marlin diet, billfish may be found wherever there are blackfin.)

Cruising the same banks and reefs is the superbly colorful dolphin—which really is shaped somewhat like a blunt-nosed cigar and may weigh anywhere from five to fifty pounds or more. And yet another member of the mackerel family inhabiting these climes is the king mackerel—also called kingfish or cavalla. Slender but powerful (and quite ferocious when hooked), a big king is likely to scale thirty pounds. On a few occasions hundred-pounders have been caught, yet it is common to try for these fish with light tackle.

As for the wahoo, my primary quarry

while I was aboard the *Coral Sea*, it, too, is a big but slender mackerel. In Bermuda waters, six-foot specimens weighing over a hundred pounds have been taken, though the average wahoo weighs about fifty pounds. The long, low dorsal fin is armed with twenty-one to twenty-seven sharp spines, and the long, tubular snout seems—when the mouth is open—to bristle with strong, flat teeth. A typically predatory mackerel, the wahoo strikes hard even when it fails to hook itself. It battles with ferocity and rewards the successful angler with fine table fare.

Then, too, there is the barracuda, even more toothy and killerlike in appearance than the wahoo. In view of the way this savage predator will attack a game fish that has been hooked, it is not surprising that the barracuda is more often killed as a pest than as a game species. But the fact remains that a good-sized barracuda is an exhilarating adversary.

Since offshore fishing is composed of valleys as well as peaks, frequently with lengthy intervals between fish, activity on a boat is either fast or slow. There is no in-between rhythm. And along about four o'clock in the afternoon, when the sun seems to invade every square inch of the cabin and the boat is rising and falling softly, it is hard to believe anything is still awake and moving out there in the sea. Then may come a sudden clatter as the line is pulled out of the snap on the outrigger and someone, Boyd most likely, shouts, "Strike!" A vivid moment. Instantly everyone is awake. I get the rod out of the holder with shaking hands and hit the fish three, four, five times. If the fish is a wahoo, I'll know soon enough by the way it behaves. Meanwhile, there is nothing I can do while the line runs out, cutting across the water at an angle to the boat. This one is a wahoo, all right. At one point far out, there is a glint of silver, like the flash of a knife blade, as the ridge of its back momentarily appears above the surface. Its speed is awesome, even slightly terrifying, and brings explosions of wonder from all. The fish is now slamming and banging through the water on a line almost parallel to the boat. The trick here is to keep pressure on it so that the weight of the water won't force the hook out of its mouth. Maneuvering the boat helps, so does a reel geared to a ratio of four to one. Pros at the game know the maximum pressure they can exert without breaking the line before they break the fish. For the rest of us it's a matter of staying well within the limits of the line, of playing safe, and for this reason it takes us longer to break a fish than it does the pros. Once you are on top of a fish—that is, once you are taking in more line than he is taking out—your contest with the fish settles down to an exercise of lifting and reeling, lifting and reeling, until it is near enough to the boat to be gaffed.

This fish weighed about fifty pounds. A steely, bluish-gray sheen covered its back, and its sides were a silvery bronze. The dark vertical markings, glowing blue bars, that are characteristic of wahoo began to fade almost as soon as it was removed from the sea. It was one of three we caught that day —a fourth threw the hook—and all of them ranged between forty and fifty pounds. These are run-of-the-mill fish by Bermuda standards, and little did we know at the time we were catching them that on another boat in the area history was being made. Fishing on *Argus* that same day and using the same 30-pound test line, G.S.C. Tatem, a Bermudian, boated a wahoo over seven feet long which weighed 108½ pounds!

Congratulations, Mr. Tatém, whoever you are. If you need a hand the next time, give a shout. I'd like to go along. Those Banks are almost as great as Whale Bay. ◉

their wheel-lock rifles, or as separate scoops in hunting pouches.

All of these factors quickly added up to real accuracy that affected sports events in many ways. Riflemen regularly aimed at deer and chamois at distances considered impossible by their friends with smoothbores. In target matches the contrast was so startling that tradition-minded shooters protested the use of the new rifles. At first, conservative marksmen resisted the winds of change and banned rifled arms completely. Target shooting, however, was a major sport in central Europe. It had afforded prestige and the chance of valuable prizes for centuries—since the days when archers had competed for the favors of a pretty maiden in the fourteenth century. Over the years the prizes had become less imaginative, but they were still highly attractive, and riflemen did not wish to be excluded. They clamored for admittance, and gradually the smooth gunners gave in. Obviously, they could not compete with the new rifles on the same terms. The only possible compromise had to be separate events—and greater ranges for the rifles, so that their scores would have some comparability.

Even if the Leipzig match of 1498, with its special category for rifles, cannot be be proved, the trend must have begun about then. During the 1500's, most shooters began to accept special rifle events during their contests. After 1560 they became common, and by 1600 they were standard for any full-fledged meet. In 1605, for instance, one of these dual meets took place at Basel, Switzerland. It is recorded that marksmen with smoothbores competed at a range of five hundred and seventy feet, using a target two-and-a-half feet in diameter. When this is contrasted with the fact that an eighteenth-century soldier with a flintlock musket rated good marks if he could hit a man-sized target at about half this distance, the skill of these marksmen of a hundred years earlier becomes impressive, indeed. And this was just for smoothbore shooters! Riflemen aimed at a 3½-foot target at the astounding distance of eight hundred and five feet. And these competitors fired offhand: They stood, holding their arms freely in front of their chests or with the stocks pressed against their cheeks. It was not yet common practice to brace the butt against the shoulder, and in fact, most rifle-butt stocks came in shapes that would have made it very uncomfortable to press them against shoulder or chest. A rifle marksman had to have arms strong enough to bear all the weight of his piece without shaking and to cope with the recoil.

Princes and potentates set great store by the talents of these keen-eyed and stout-armed competitors. They felt that a citizenry strong in competent marksmen offered an important asset in time of war. Thus they encouraged both gunners and riflemen to hone their skills, even providing a quota of free ammunition for practice, and they often paid the costs of major target matches. Such competitions, they believed, served two useful purposes. They encouraged the men to practice shooting, while also playing a role in international understanding and promoting the cause of peace. For the big matches, the planners invited competitors from all over central Europe, regardless of nationality or allegiance. Traveling to and from such shoots, the marksmen and their supporters came to know people and places in other states and principalities and to understand them. Friendships developed, and the cause of peace profited, the rulers believed.

The rifle these peaceful marksmen fired was the direct ancestor of the jaeger. The design change that brought forth the newer rifle began about 1665 or 1670. First, the new French-style flintlock began to replace the standard wheel lock. This new lock did not fire as quickly as the old one, but it was much simpler to make and repair, and it could be readied for shooting much faster. The second major change came in the design of the butt stock. This important area became broader, and it dropped off slightly from the old straight line. The butt plate, too, acquired a smooth face without knobs or other sharp projections. Now a shooter could brace the broad smooth butt against his shoulder, while the slight drop in the stock brought the barrel up to a convenient height for aiming. This offered a much steadier hold that improved the long-range shooting so necessary in hunting deer and chamois. It also helped prevent the cuts and bruises of the face that could easily result if a rifleman failed to hold a cheek butt tightly enough. When these changes reached their full development, the jaeger arrived upon the scene. The new jaeger rifle began to compete with the wheel lock shortly before 1700, even though some tradition-minded Germans clung to the old wheel lock and the straight cheek stock until after 1750. By 1725 the older form had become an anachronism, valued only by conservatives who prized the wheel lock.

The flintlock and the new butt design set the jaeger rifle apart from its predecessors, but the new rifle had other important characteristics as well. For one thing it was a short piece, usually with an octagonal barrel between twenty-four and thirty inches long. Its bore was big, averaging between .60 and .75, for it took considerable striking power to drop a wild boar or one of the other larger animals of the region. The rifling that spun the big bullets from such bores was deep and multigrooved. Usually there were from seven to nine of these grooves spiraling in a relatively slow twist. Sights consisted of an open V at the rear and a blade at the front.

A further aid to accurate long-range shooting lay in the set, or hair, trigger normally found on these rifles. The strong mainsprings of flintlock rifles required a hard pull to release the sear, and this made it difficult for all but the strongest-fingered marksmen to hold a steady aim. With the double set triggers found on most jaegers, the marksman first pulled one fairly stiff trigger to set the mechanism, then fired with the second trigger that required only a touch and so would not disturb his aim. A broad trigger guard protected these delicate triggers and also had a rear extension to provide a firm grip for the three rear fingers.

Another noteworthy characteristic of the jaeger was a small rectangular box carved into the right side of the butt stock. A sliding cover of wood, bone, ivory, or horn with a spring catch closed this receptacle and made it a convenient place to carry small tools or an extra flint. European shooters apparently did not use it to carry their greased patches as later American riflemen did. Thus, the usual term for this box in England is "butt trap" instead of the American "patch box."

Most surviving jaeger rifles are finely made and beautifully decorated. The workmanship shows skill and precision. Even hidden surfaces are smoothed and polished. Inletting is crisp and tight. The decoration almost always includes relief carving, and frequently there is metal, bone, or ivory inlay that may be further enhanced by engraving, dyeing, chiseling, or gilding. Barrels, trigger guards, butt plates, and other metal parts may also be engraved, chiseled, blued, and gilded. Yet in most cases this decoration is subservient to function. The rifle remains a sturdy weapon that shoots well. Sometimes, however, the decoration is the most important if not the only reason for the rifle. Such rifles are great rarities, designed as cabinet pieces or ostentatious gifts, and they include such hard-to-imagine features as barrels of solid silver,

which would have been too soft for service, or glass, which would have shattered. George IV of England had a jaeger rifle made by Jacob Walster of Saarbrücken about 1760; it boasted a heart-shaped bore and a barrel that twisted to give the effect of rifling. This spectacular rifle even had a twisted ramrod that the shooter could literally screw down the bore.

Many jaegers, however, were simple guns, well-made but plain. These were the arms of the professional foresters, gamekeepers, and soldiers. The foresters and gamekeepers never accounted for a great many of the short rifles, but soldiers brought them to world fame. Riflemen quickly appeared in armies throughout much of Europe. Early in the 1600's, even before the development of the jaeger, King Christian IV of Denmark had begun to recruit riflemen for his army. The jaeger offered an even better rifled arm, and as early as 1715 ski troops in Norway adopted it as a standard weapon. Great Britain utilized jaeger riflemen in some of the continental wars of the eighteenth century and even equipped a few troops with them for special purposes in America during the French and Indian War of 1755-1763. When the American Revolution broke out a few years later, Great Britain again

Left: Unsigned jaeger rifle, c. 1750, is attributed to Stockmar family of Suhl, court gunmakers to Elector of Saxony. Below: Stockmar lock and barrel decoration is characterized by superbly chiseled steel on gilt background. Barrel is also etched to resemble damascus twist.

turned to these fine rifles and hired military marksmen from Anspach-Bayreuth, Hesse-Cassel, Hesse-Hanau, and Brunswick to fignt across the Atlantic. As late as the siege of Yorktown, in October of 1781, Lieutenant Colonel St. George Tucker of the Virginia militia was unprepared for the way in which the Anspach riflemen picked off his men at a considerable distance—and in the dusk, when visibility was poor.

After the Revolution, the jaeger continued to spread its influence. It offered a primary inspiration for the design of Great Britain's notable Baker rifle. It actually influenced the Model 1803 American military rifle and its successors as late as the 1860's. And the same was true for sporting rifles in Europe, if not in America. Traces of the jaeger heritage can even be discerned in the longer, slender Kentucky rifles. On the Continent, the short, big-bore rifle with a butt trap—the jaeger—remained the standard pattern as long as hunters used muzzle-loaders for their sport. For more than a hundred and fifty years, in flintlock or percussion, from the Atlantic to the Urals and even in America, this great gun fostered accurate shooting. It helped to create a tradition of marksmanship that its breechloading and repeating successors still maintain. ◉

can be bought across the counter at reasonable prices, yet untold thousands of shooters labor into the night with all manner of esoteric equipment and supplies: levering loading presses, adjusting dies, weighing powder charges, resizing cases, even making their own bullets on special tools. They do this knowing they can simply buy good ammunition for anything from squirrels to elephants.

Some riflemen (as well as some handgunners and shotgunners) may honestly feel that economy would be reason enough to justify such effort. There are also those who are simply—no, obsessively—inquisitive, and who want to know everything possible about the inner workings of ammunition. But I think they are outnumbered by those of us who are quixotic dreamers. And there is a special breed of quixotic devotee who specializes in some particular form of shooting or hunting wherein even the finest factory ammunition does not quite meet the highest standards. That's when handloading can really pay off.

An addict may well spend more time loading and experimenting than shooting. Like the record-seeking trophy hunter or the dry-fly purist, he begins marching to a different drum. Epitomizing the type is John Buhmiller, sixtyish and gray, an elephant hunter extraordinary. I can easily picture him as he eased his big .450 Magnum rifle to his shoulder and squeezed off a shot that felled his twenty-fifth elephant of the year. John is no game hog, and every one of those tuskers was legal. He was assisting the government of Tanzania (then Tanganyika) in elephant-control work. Not only did he have the satisfaction of knowing that the rifle with which he dropped the world's largest land animal so efficiently had been made by his own hand, but the ammunition was also his own creation. Handloaded with great attention to detail in his own little shop, it contained special bullets designed for the quickest possible one-shot kills.

A retired rifle-barrel maker of considerable repute, Buhmiller had long been dissatisfied with commercially available ammunition for dangerous African game. The only way to improve performance was to handload his own ammunition. The big .45-caliber, soft-point bullets didn't give the penetration required; the one full-jacketed make that was strong enough to penetrate without deformation had a nose shape that sometimes caused it to veer off its path during penetration. And bullets with the right shape were too lightly constructed to penetrate deeply enough.

After trying everything the factories offered, John decided that if he could reshape the steel-jacketed Winchester 500-grain .458 "solid" bullet properly, he could ensure straight penetration and more shock upon impact. He made dies to reshape the point to wadcutter form—making the bullet a cylinder in profile—but with the forward portion of reduced diameter to ride over the lands of the rifling.

Similar reshaping, or swaging, is fairly common practice among handloaders with lightly constructed bullets, but it presents problems when jackets are of tough steel and over 1/16-inch thick. He tried other approaches, including different point shapes, and even reversing the bullet in the case so that its sharp-cornered flat base struck the target first, cutting a clean hole and delivering maximum shock. Dozens of different reworked bullets were fired at various velocities into dry wood. Those that performed best contained a conical cavity in the nose.

Unfortunately, in reshaping the bullets to get the desired performance, a feeding problem was created. The cylindrical .458 Winchester Magnum case would not feed reliably for those essential, fast repeat shots

Behind muzzle brakes of .450 Magnums is target with single-hole, 3/4-inch group made by three 350-grain Hornady bullets.

when loaded with squared-off bullets. The problem was solved temporarily by using the much larger bottleneck .460 Weatherby case. But this required a very large, heavy Magnum action, and the case capacity was much too great to operate efficiently at the velocity levels John desired. This problem was solved by shortening the big case to the length of the .458 Winchester and bottlenecking it to provide perfect feeding. He thus created a wildcat cartridge ideally suited to his purposes and not available anywhere else.

Not everyone hunts elephants by the dozens, but everyone who does seek big or dangerous game can certainly benefit from John's experience. Following his lead in handloading specifically for one type of game not only improves performance but increases one's pleasure in the sport.

Moreover, even with today's highly uniform production methods, each rifle demands loading experimentation for best performance. Occasionally a shooter may take a new rifle directly from the box, load it with factory ammunition, and get minute-of-angle accuracy. Or it may be that he can obtain the same results by merely picking any appropriate handload from one of the reloading manuals. On the other hand, the very next rifle of the same model, coming off the same production line, may refuse to shoot better than five- or six-inch groups with the same ammunition.

The basic approach to the attainment of accuracy and power may be fairly constant, but the exceptionally knowledgeable rifleman often modifies that approach slightly (nevertheless significantly) on the basis of his experience plus his specific goal for a cartridge. I can easily find examples among my own experiments. I once obtained a very nice Newton rifle which had been originally in .256 caliber, but had been rebored to .30/06. It was an excellent sporter for big game, and it shot passably well with 150- and 220-grain loads, but, in spite of being very carefully bedded and in fine mechanical shape, it simply would not deliver adequate accuracy with factory 180-grain ammunition. Since this was the weight I wished to use, it was necessary to work up my own hunting load.

I selected three makes of bullets whose accuracy and performance had pleased me in other game rifles. Three powders suitable for use with those bullets were chosen, and ten cartridges loaded with each powder behind each bullet. Powder-charge weights were chosen to produce standard factory-load ballistics. Those ninety rounds were then fired in five-shot groups, slowly and carefully, and under conditions as nearly identical as possible.

Of the nine different loads, two showed a significant edge in accuracy over the others. Additional cartridges were then loaded with those bullet-powder combinations, varying the charge slightly above and below the charge first used. Further test firing disclosed that one of these combinations (a 180-grain Nosler bullet and 56.6 grains of IMR 4350 powder) produced measurably better accuracy than any of the others. As a matter of fact, it made cold-barrel three-shot groups of 1-3/8 inches at a hundred yards, and even at twice that range the bullet holes covered no more than three inches of target area.

Certainly this is highly satisfactory accuracy for any big-game hunting. The significant point is that it was obtained by handloading for a barrel which would do no better than four inches at a hundred yards with the very best of factory-loaded ammunition. Furthermore, this performance was obtained with a bullet superbly suited to the largest species of North American game.

Aside from the selection of components to meet such specific requirements, reloading is simple, yet it demands enough concentration and encompasses a sufficient variety of loads to be thoroughly enjoyable. After setting up the proper dies and press, and a powder scale, my procedure is to wash and dry or wipe clean the fired case. Then I lightly lubricate the outside with a minute film of lanolin or prepared case lubricant. I remove sharp edges at the case mouth and then run each case into the resizing die, which is adjusted as specified by the maker. The single resizing step reduces the case to proper dimensions, expels the fired primer, and expands the neck back to the proper diameter to maintain a tight grip on the bullet. Most presses have a provision for seating a fresh primer as the case is withdrawn from the die, so this is done next. I then wipe the lubricant off the case with a cloth moistened with lighter fluid or solvent. Next I weigh out the correct powder charge on the scale and funnel it into the case. The bullet-seating die is now placed in the press and adjusted. Bullets are started straight in the cases by hand, after which I run each round into the seating die to complete the job. *Voilà!* My own ammunition, not available anywhere else.

Further development of a basic load consists of varying one factor at a time (powder type and amount, bullet make and weight, etc.) until the desired performance level is attained. The importance of chronographing has been debated, but obviously if you wish to duplicate a factory load or reach a specified level, you'll require the use of a chronograph to measure actual velocities. Most important during load development is a constant alertness for any evidence of excessive pressures—for example, primer distortion, difficult extraction, undue recoil. Any such evidence calls for immediate reduction of the powder charge.

The same loading techniques—but with refinements—are of value to the rifleman for other purposes than hunting. Take target competition, for example. The kind of accuracy that was needed by Buhmiller, impressive though it was for a very large caliber, wouldn't get a shooter past the parking lot at a benchrest match. In that game, the marksman uses equipment that only remotely resembles a sporting rifle, and that may often weigh over forty pounds. Such exotic guns are sometimes literally carved from solid metal by the owners or by their favorite gunsmiths. They have massive stocks flattened or fluted at fore-end and butt to rest solidly and squarely on supports that may range from shaped sandbags to elaborate mechanical systems resembling the cradle of an artillery carriage.

The goal of this game is to place ten bullets into the smallest group possible at ranges of one, two, and three hundred yards. Groups generally form just one ragged hole in the target, and it is necessary to use a moving strip behind the targets to prove that ten bullets actually went through that tiny ragged hole. Groups measuring under 1/4 inch are not uncommon at two hundred yards, and the records at that distance run considerably smaller.

The men (and frequently women) who undertake this uniquely difficult type of shooting must, of course, be perfectionists to whom the end justifies the means. Many are professional types who unwind by immersing their minds and bodies in the game. No small number are gunsmiths and engineers in the arms industry. Others are ordinary people in all walks of life who find an outlet and a goal in seeking the perfect one-hole group. The benchrest shooter couldn't care less how well his bullet would penetrate or expand on game. His only concern is consistent accuracy of a degree hitherto considered impossible of attainment. Nothing but meticulously handloaded ammunition can even be considered.

In producing such ammunition, one must carefully select and inspect every component. In many instances, this means measuring and weighing and minutely examining every case in a lot of a hundred or more to select perhaps only twenty of the most uniform cases possible. These will be subjected to modification by fire-forming (being fired to expand and fit the chamber perfectly), and a careful reaming of the flash hole—not to mention trimming and reaming the necks for maximum concentricity. Some shooters even go so far as to file or scratch an index mark on the head of each case to insure that they can be returned to the chamber with the same orientation for each firing.

The benchrester must select primers from those commercially available, though he does so by careful inspection and, sometimes, weighing and measuring. Individual guns may achieve slightly better accuracy with a particular make of primer. Powder, too, is limited to what is commercially available. The benchrester selects the type most suitable to his particular cartridge and most productive in his gun. Then he concentrates upon uniformity of charge, even to its distribution in the case at the time of firing.

But he lavishes his greatest attention upon the bullet, for in spite of the importance of the other components, this remains by far the most decisive factor in the ultimate accuracy of ammunition. He may decide, like Buhmiller, that nothing produced by the factories is quite good enough. Winning shooters do use factory bullets with a reasonable degree of frequency, but I've noticed that the more meticulous subject them first to very close scrutiny and testing. Those who make their own bullets, and go about the job seriously, use dies and gauges made to a degree of precision found only in the finest of instruments. They may well begin with nothing but the raw copper-alloy bullet jacket, which is trimmed and reamed or bored in a special fixture to tolerances of 1/10,000th of an inch. Then the lead cores are cut, preformed, and weighed, preseated in the cups, and the assembly is carefully processed through bullet-forming dies in a heavy-duty press. The completed bullet is tested, weighed, and measured and may be produced in minor variations of form, weight, and location of center of gravity to attain maximum accuracy in a particular rifle barrel.

Aside from pure hunting and pure accuracy, there is another area of great handloading interest prompted by the current tendency to combine arms collecting and shooting. No longer are valuable pieces invariably relegated to a display cabinet; the shootable ones are often shot. Many a gun buff owns one or several unusual guns for which ammunition is no longer available. Without cartridges they obviously can't be shot or used for hunting, but when properly fed they are as effective as ever.

A skilled shooter is likely to feel a strong

sensation when he holds a fine example of the classic double rifle—one of those superbly executed sculptures in wood and metal that emanated from old British gunmaking houses such as Purdey or Holland & Holland. One examines such an arm with reverence, and one has a keen yearning to shoot it. Some of the older hammerless models, elegantly chased and engraved and so closely fitted that parts move upon each other like oiled glass, would cost $5,000 or more to duplicate today. It is improbable that their like will be made again. To own such a rifle may be a joy, but if it cannot be supplied with reliable cartridges, a tinge of sadness will accompany the glow.

Fortunately, anyone with a reasonable amount of loading experience and the willingness to obtain special dies and components can make up ammunition for almost any of the fine double or Express rifles, even though original cases and bullets may not have been manufactured for years.

Custom-made bullets, as well as dies and equipment to make one's own in almost any diameter and weight, may be obtained from several sources that advertise in various shooting publications. Often it is possible to obtain a reasonable supply of serviceable fired cases of the correct caliber. If given proper care, they will last for many years. Loading data can be found in several sources, notably *Cartridges of the World*, published by the Gun Digest Company, and *Cartridge Conversions*, published by Stackpole. The *NRA Illustrated Reloading Hand-*

Remington benchrest .222, topped by 20X scope, is shown with Redding powder scale, chamfering tool, and loading manual.

book is also an excellent source. The special Berdan primers required for the old British cartridges can be obtained from Alcan, Stoeger Arms, and Oregon Ammunition Service.

However, if original cases are not available, or as a hedge against undue deterioration of those obtained, it is usually possible to reshape another existing case to fit. For example, Rigby produced a number of fine double rifles for its .400/350 Magnum cartridge. Original cases are virtually collectors' items, though standard .35 (.357-.358-inch) bullets may be used. A little research discloses that the 2-3/4-inch-long Rigby case is virtually identical in head and rim dimensions to the 9.3x74R, still manufactured in Europe and imported into the United States. Only minor alterations are necessary to make it fit the Rigby chamber. Reduce the neck diameter in a .35 Whelen or .35 Winchester resizing die to hold .357-.358-inch bullets, and set the shoulder back slightly during the process. Firing with a medium-weight bullet and a moderate charge of smokeless powder will fire-form the case to fit the chamber perfectly. From that point onward, the re-formed case may be safely reloaded to reasonable performance almost innumerable times in normal fashion.

In addition to British doubles, many other fine firearms are chambered for obsolete cartridges, and sometimes a handloader can convert ammunition of another caliber to the needed dimensions. Several years ago a good friend of mine, Leslie Fields, obtained a very fine Rigby Mauser magazine rifle chambered for the .350 Rimless Magnum, but ammunition was not available. A study of specimen cartridges and dimensional data tables disclosed that, with some work, we could reform .375 H&H Magnum brass to fit the Rigby chamber. This was done by first turning off the headspacing belt, leaving the rim and extractor groove at their original dimensions, necking the case down to accept .357-diameter bullets, trimming the case to a length of 2.74 inches, then pushing the shoulder back carefully until the formed case would headspace properly upon it in the chamber of that particular rifle. Fire-forming with a moderate load completed the job, producing readily reloadable, Boxer-primed cases.

A shooter-collector may acquire a fine gun of much older vintage, and he need not be daunted in his desire to shoot even some black-powder rifles. Perhaps he has one chambered for the .577/500 No. 2 Express or some similar cartridge which is no longer produced. But the .577 Nitro Express three-inch cartridge is still available. Its case may be shortened to the proper 2.8-inch length, necked down to .50 caliber, then loaded for use in the No. 2 Express chamber. Unfortunately, not all such conversions are quite that simple. For example, the .416 Rigby (usually found in Rigby magazine rifles, though occasionally in double rifles) requires that the .378 or .460 Weatherby case be lathe-turned to proper shape and size at the head before being reshaped and shortened to the proper length. A bit more complicated procedure than the previous examples, but certainly worthwhile in order to put a classic gun back into operation.

If sufficient research is done (and *Cartridges of the World*, available at most gun shops, is an excellent place to begin studying), there is hardly a gun for which ammunition cannot be produced from reasonably available components. There are still some handloaders who will excuse their obsession on the basis of economy, but they, too, are secretly caught up in the quest. They know that handloading for special purposes can produce performance and satisfaction and availability—perhaps even a glimmering of elusive perfection—that cannot be reduced to a question of price.

sportsman afterthoughts

Arie deZanger's cover photograph for this issue shows lures and reels made during the decade after World War I, important years in the development of modern bait-casting tools and techniques. At right center is a Horton Blue Grass #3 reel, which is very close in design to earlier Meek models. The reel attached to a rod is the famous Pflueger Supreme of 1920. At bottom right is a black and white jointed Jim Tracy plug with three single hooks, made in 1918. The Al Foss weedless Shimmy Wiggler (top row, center) and the renowned black and white Eppinger Dardevle spoon (left of the Horton reel) appeared in 1920. Among great plugs that have hardly changed is the perch-scale-finished 1921 Creek Chub Pikie Minnow (top right). The lures are from the collections of Lee Wulff and Jim Salvato.

In connection with his many fishing and hunting trips to remote areas, **Jerome B. Robinson** ("Salmon and Caribou of the Ungava," p. 12) reports that he is frequently asked for addresses of recommended camp operators. Sportsmen who wish to follow his trail to the DePas River camp in northern Quebec should make reservations long in advance through the Montagnais Club, Box 112, Sept Iles, Quebec. The weekly rate is $475, including the guide's fee, meals, and the flight from Schefferville.

Although Robinson is in his early thirties, he is an old hand at reporting on outdoor sports in wilderness areas from the Arctic to the tropics. His articles have appeared in a variety of publications, from *Reader's Digest* to *Outdoor Life*. At press time he is covering the National Bird Dog Championships in Grand Junction, Tennessee, together with **Hanson Carroll,** who took the photographs for the Ungava story.

Since Carroll raises and trains English pointers, he has a special interest in attending the southern field trials, where this breed predominates. His outdoor photographs have been published in a number of magazines, including *Life*, *Look*, and *Sports Illustrated*. He and Robinson often work as a team.

Another wildlife photographer, **Jack Gates,** worked with author **George Bird Evans** in preparing "Leaves of a Gunner's Diary" (p. 36). At press time Gates, too, is in the South—in Georgia, hunting quail with the well-known sportsman-industrialist-conservationist Al Rockwell. He specializes in photographing wildlife so that he can often work in the uplands, "where any sensible man would want to be."

In addition to photographs, the "Diary" illustrations include sketches by the author. George Evans was a popular magazine illustrator from 1938 to 1947 (with time out to serve in the Navy during the Second World War). He then began his rather unusual version of retirement—hunting, raising a highly reputed strain of setters, and writing books in collaboration with his wife Kay. In addition to a novel entitled *The Pink Carrara*, about life in New York, the Evanses have produced four suspense novels. Connoisseurs of this genre will remember their best-known book, *Hawk Watch*.

"Mysteries of the Loading Bench" (p. 60) is by a man famous for his familiarity with those mysteries. **George C. Nonte** is the author of *Cartridge Conversions*, a standard handloading reference and probably the best-known of his technical writings. Four other Nonte books are currently in print, and his *Book of the Air Gun* is scheduled for fall publication by Stackpole.

Major Nonte has been fishing and hunting since he was a small boy in Illinois, and not even his twenty-year Army career seriously interfered with his avocation. (He retired in 1964 to devote full time to writing, and last year alone he published a hundred and fifty magazine articles.) He was stationed in a number of foreign lands, and hunted in all of them. In Iran, he once found himself surrounded by five exceptionally large Russian boars. The species abounds there and is rarely hunted in a Moslem country where pork is not eaten. Armed with a slow-firing bolt-action Mauser, he could not chance shooting one of the animals and perhaps bringing on a charge by the others—so he stood perfectly still until the band wandered away.

Russ Carpenter (Campfire Cookery," p. 80) has been collecting trail-cooking secrets for many years. In the Forties, when he was a tool and die maker, he began repairing guns as a hobby, soon earning so great a reputation that he became a gunsmith. His writing career also began during this period, when he devoted more and more time to hunting and fishing, often in the company of the late Larry Koller, who was known for his skill with a skillet as well as for his outdoor writings.

Carpenter and Koller were in sad agreement about the quality of most camp cooking, and both men eventually became expert outdoor chefs in self-defense.